ALADDIN

ALADDIN

A Pantomime

by Chris Denys and Chris Harris

JOSEF WEINBERGER PLAYS

LONDON

ALADDIN
First published in 2001
by Josef Weinberger Ltd
12-14 Mortimer Street, London, W1T 3JJ

Copyright © 2001 by Chris Denys and Chris Harris
Copyright © 1992 by Chris Denys and Chris Harris as an unpublished dramatic composition

The authors assert their moral right to be identified as the authors of the work.

ISBN 0 85676 252 0

This play is protected by Copyright. According to Copyright Law, no public performance or reading of a protected play or part of that play may be given without prior authorization from Josef Weinberger Plays, as agent for the Copyright Owners.

From time to time it is necessary to restrict or even withdraw the rights of certain plays. **It is therefore essential to check with us before making a commitment to produce a play.**

NO PERFORMANCE MAY BE GIVEN WITHOUT A LICENCE

AMATEUR PRODUCTIONS
Royalties are due at least fourteen days prior to the first performance. A royalty quotation will be issued upon receipt of the following details:

Name of Licensee
Play Title
Place of Performance
Dates and Number of Performances
Audience Capacity
Ticket Prices

PROFESSIONAL PRODUCTIONS
All enquiries regarding stock and repertory rights should be addressed to Josef Weinberger Ltd., 12-14 Mortimer Street, London W1T 3JJ. Enquiries for all other rights should be addressed to the authors, c/o Josef Weinberger Ltd.

OVERSEAS PRODUCTIONS
Applications for productions overseas should be addressed to our local authorised agents. Further details are listed in our catalogue of plays, published every two years, or available from Josef Weinberger Plays at the address above.

CONDITIONS OF SALE
This book is sold subject to the condition that it shall not by way of trade or otherwise be resold, hired out, circulated or distributed without prior consent of the Publisher. **Reproduction of the text either in whole or part and by any means is strictly forbidden.**

Printed by Watkiss Studios Limited, Biggleswade England

This Pantomime of **ALADDIN** was first produced by the Bristol Old Vic Company at the Theatre Royal, Bristol on December 4th 1992 with the following cast:

ABANAZAR	Mark Buffery
THYLVIA, SLAVE OF THE RING	Heather Williams
WISHEE WASHEE	Patrick Miller
PING	Anthony Venditti
PONG	Robert Beach
ALADDIN	Simone Bendix
PRINCESS JASMINE	Sara Markland
WIDOW TWANKEE	Chris Harris
THE JINI OF THE LAMP	Anthony Venditti
THE EMPEROR OF CHINA	Robert Beach
THE PEKINESE	The Dancers of ACRODANCE 2000

Directed by Chris Dennys
Designed by Mick Bearwash
Music Supervised by Neil Rhoden
Musical Direction by John O'Hara
Choreography by Gail Gordon
Lighting Designed by Tim Streader
Sound Designed by Mark Gallagher

CHARACTERS

ABANAZAR	Evil Magician and sometime Bandit
THYLVIA	The Slave of the Ring, and a Very Good Fairy
WISHEE WASHEE	Widow Twankee's Assistant
PRINCESS JASMINE	
PING	of the Pekin Palace Police
PONG	also of the Pekin Palace Police
ALADDIN	The Hero
WIDOW TRANKEE	His Mother
THE JINI OF THE LAMP	
THE EMPEROR OF CHINA	
THE PEKINESE	Poor people of Pekin

SCENES

ACT ONE

Prologue:	(*In front of Panto Gauze*)
Scene 1:	THE PEKIN MUNICIPAL PARK
Scene 2:	A STREET IN OLD PEKIN
Scene 3:	WIDOW TWANKEE'S LAUNDRY
Scene 4:	A STREET IN OLD PEKIN
Scene 5:	THE MOUNTAINS OF HOWAANGAWAWAHAAAH
Scene 6:	THE CAVERN OF THE WONDERFUL LAMP
Scene 7:	A STREET IN OLD PEKIN
Scene 8:	WIDOW TWANKEE'S KITCHEN

ACT TWO

Prologue:	(*In front of Panto Guaze*)
Scene 1:	PEKIN MUNICIPAL PARK
Scene 2:	THE IMPERIAL PRISON
Scene 3:	THE DUNGEON OF ALADDIN'S PALACE (*Now in the Sahara*)
Scene 4:	A STREET IN OLD PEKIN
Scene 5:	PEKIN MUNICIPAL PARK
Scene 6:	A STREET IN OLD PEKIN
Scene 7:	THE BALLROOM OF THE IMPERIAL PALACE

AUTHORS' NOTE

This Pantomime is intended to be "traditional" in that the Principal Boy is a girl, the Dame is a man, the story is told clearly with as much action and knock-about as possible and, very importantly, it is local to the town or city in which it is performed. It's also meant to be great fun – both for the audience and for those who perform and present it.

The local references in this script relate to Bristol – where it was first produced in 1992 and again in 1997 before transferring to Cheltenham in 1998 (where it acquired references to Lansdown, Little Herberts and Up Hatherly) so please feel free to localise as necessary and desirable.

Also, the staging is as described because we were working in beautifully equipped theatres with excellent design and production departments able to give us anything we asked for. It doesn't have to be like that, of course, and can be adapted to how much – or how little – you have at your disposal.

The stage directions, groundplans and indicated lighting, sound, follow-spot and pyrotechnic cues are only intended as suggestions and not to be in any way prescriptive.

The only sort of "flash" units allowed by Fire Officers these days are ruinously expensive and we always wrote our scripts with a liberal use of these effects only to cut them back to essentials when we saw what it was going to cost.

The Music:
Pantomime audiences do like to know the tunes so we have always used either current and perennial favourites as written or taken well-known melodies and written lyrics which stand as part of the plot and move the story along.

Some of the music we have used is out of copyright (eg, the Act One Finale is set to the Trio from Act Five of Gounod's "Faust" and is clear) *but other melodies are still **in** copyright and you will need to pay for these if you use them through the **Performing Rights Society*** (who offer a special – and very reasonable – deal for Pantomimes).

Mostly, though, we have found that producers prefer to choose their own music to suit and show off the particular voices of their cast.

ACT ONE

Prologue

*In front of Panto Gauze. Thunder (**SQ.1**) and Lightning (**LXQ.1**). A Flash (**PyroQ.1.**) and ABANAZAR appears DL. (**FSQ.1.**)*

ABANAZAR: Greetings, churls!
And boys and girls!
It's your neighbourhood magician.
Abanazar's the name –
And evil's the game –
I'm a fiend with one ambition:
To be the curse
Of the Universe –
Master of all I survey –
From Pekin Town
To Bedminster Down,
You'll be my slaves – O yea!
And nothing could be finer
Than to start in Pekin, China
Where Aladdin, a regular scamp –
Is the only heir –
Though he ain't aware –
To a Jini what lives in a lamp.
Aladdin's Dad
Was a bit of a lad –
Up to any old hanky panky –
Shiftless and lazy
And three parts crazy
And known as Hoo Flung Twankee.
But it seems that he'd
Done one good deed
For, once, in a fearful blizzard,
He came across,
Sick, tired and lost,
A clapped-out wandering wizard.
The poor old guy
Was about to die –
In the wilderness forsaken
When along came Hoo –
Who knoo what to do –
And he saved the wizard's bacon.
The grateful chap
Gave Hoo Flung this map
(*He unrolls a long, cloth map – not unlike a toilet roll.*)
So Aladdin could find the cave

ACT ONE

> Where there's jewels and gold
> And a lamp which holds
> A Jini to be his slave.
> But Aladdin's due
> And, as I slew Hoo,
> For the lamp I'll banjax the lad.
> And once I win it –
> With the Jini in it,
> I'll be ever so – ever so – BAD!

(*A Flash.* (**PyroQ.2; LXQ.2; FSQ.2.**) *THYLVIA appears DR.*)

THYLVIA: Oh no you won't!

ABANAZAR: O yes I will!

THYLVIA: (*Leading the AUDIENCE*) Oh no you won't!

ABANAZAR: Oh yes I . . .

THYLVIA: Well, wait and thee!
(*To AUDIENCE.*) It'th little me –
Thylvia, Thlave of the Wing.
I twail cloudth of happineth
And, occathionally, thing. (*Sings.*) Laaaaa!
(*To ABANAZAR.*) I'll thwart your thinithter thchemeth you
wetch,

Although I'm jutht a thlave,
I'm twuthty, twue –
Not at all like you –
And weally wather bwave.
And tho, thly thlug, I tell you
That the cavern ith enchanted
Wherein the gold and jewelth
And the wonderful lamp are planted
And none may enter nor yet come near
Thave for Aladdin in his eighteenth year.

ABANAZAR: Alright, I heard,
You fairy nerd.
Why else d'you think I'm here?
Why have I hitched from the hot Saharah
But to lure the lad from the straight and narrah.
He's eighteen today and in my trap he'll tumble.

THYLVIA: If you enter that cave, the woof will cwumble
And, ere you can thteal the lamp, you thlimy wat,

	The cavern will collapthe and cwuth you flat.
ABANAZAR:	But you, "Thylvia", are trapped in a worthless ring. Unless the ring is rubbed, you can't do anything. You're powerless. A prisoner. Can't help him with your magic.
THYLVIA:	That'th twue! O poo! I hope thith panto don't end up twagic. (*To the AUDIENCE.*) Will you help me? Will you be my fwiendth? And thave Aladdin fwom a thticky end? Well. If ever he findth the wing wherein I dwell, You mutht theout out "Wub it" – "Wub it!" – that'll bweak the thpell. "Wub it! Wub it!" Come on, twy . . . (*They do.*) (*Doubtfully.*) Well, I 'thpect you'll get the hang of it by and by. Then I can uthe my magic. I've a twick or two, you know. I wath vewy nearly on the Paul Danielth' Magic Theow.
ABANAZAR:	Ha! You and this drab rabble can do your pathetic best. But the foolish youth, Aladdin will fetch the lamp at my request. I'll say I'm a long-lost relative – one of the Twankees of Ghaza. And he'll be pleased to help me then – his loving Uncle . . . Abanazar!
	(*Thunder.* (**SQ.2; LXQ.3; FSQ.1A**) *ABANAZAR exits DL, cackling nastily.*)
THYLVIA:	Oh cwumbth. I feel tho powerleth – thtuck in an antique wing. We'd better thee what'th happening in the Munithipal Park, Pekin!
(**FSQ2A**)	(*THYLVIA exits DR as lights dissolves through the Gauze* (**LXQ.4**) *to reveal a tableau of:*)

Scene One

Pekin Municipal Park. The Gauze flies out. (**FlyQ.1; LXQ.5**)

Song: ROUND AND ROUND THE PAGODAS (*PING, PONG and PEKINESE*)

ROUND AND ROUND THE PAGODAS,
FOLLOWING EV'RY TRAIL
THROUGH THE SNOW AND HAIL,
OVER HILL AND DALE.
ROUND AND ROUND THE PAGODAS,
PICTURE OUR DISTRESS –
WE'VE SEARCHED FOR HOURS
AMONG THE FLOWERS
BUT CAN'T FIND OUR PRINCESS.
EV'RYTHING WOULD BE LOVERLEY, LOVERLEY
IF WE KNEW – WHERE SHE'S TO –
MORNING, NOON AND NIGHT WE'RE ON THE GO
SO!
ROUND AND ROUND THE PAGODAS, SEARCHING
EV'RYWHERE –
IF ONLY WE HAD NOTHING TO DO WITH TIME TO
STAND AND STARE.

(*ALADDIN enters UC.*) (**FSQ.3**)

ALADDIN: Hello, everybody.

ALL: Aladdin!

PING: Did you find our Jasmine?

PONG: Did you find the Princess?

ALADDIN: I wouldn't tell you if I had. But no. I've searched the whole city without success.

(*Sings.*) UP AND DOWN, ALL OVER TOWN, I'VE
SEARCHED BOTH EAST AND WEST.
I'VE LOOKED IN EV'RY PLACE –
BUT I HAVEN'T FOUND A TRACE.
I'VE COMBED THE STREETS AND ALLEYWAYS AND I'M
WORRIED, I CONFESS,
UNTIL I SEE MY BRIDE-TO-BE. SO WILL YOU HELP ME?

ALL: YES (*All repeat chorus.*)

(*WISHEE WASHEE enters UC.*) (**FSQ.3A**)

WISHEE: E-O. (*To the AUDIENCE.*) E-O! 38 Queens Walk

ALL: E-O, Wishee Washee.

WISHEE: Who'd like some clever sweets?

ALADDIN: Clever sweets?

WISHEE: (*Throwing them to the AUDIENCE*) Smarties.

ALADDIN: You're supposed to be looking for the Princess.

WISHEE: I *was* looking for the Princess. But then I had to help this chicken what was sitting on a axe.

ALADDIN: Why was a chicken sitting on an axe?

WISHEE: She was trying to hatchet.

ALL: GROAN.

WISHEE: (*To the AUDIENCE*) They get worse. (*Sings.*)
MY NAME IS WISHEE WASHEE – I'M ALADDIN'S BESTEST CHUM.
I'M SEARCHING WITH THE REST
TO FIND THE LOST PRINCESS
I'VE DELVED ALL THROUGH THE DOCKLAND AND THE HARBOUR I HAVE SWUM
I'VE COVERED ALL OF THE CHINESE WALL
BUT I FELL AND HURT MY BUM.
SO:

(*All sing chorus.*)

(*PRINCESS JASMINE enters, furtively, UC.*) **(FSQ.3B)**

JASMINE: (*Whispering*) Aladdin . . .

ALADDIN: (*Whispering*) Princess!

WISHEE/PEKINESE: (*Aloud*) Princess Jasmine!

PING/PONG: (*Looking off L and R*) Where?

JASMINE: Ssshhh!

ALADDIN: We couldn't find you anywhere. Why were you hiding from us?

JASMINE: I wasn't hiding from you . . .

PING/PONG: (*Seeing her*) Ah hah! (*They seize her.*)

JASMINE: I was hiding from them. They make my life a misery.

        I LONG TO BE ALL FANCY FREE – TO DO JUST AS I PLEASE.
        BUT, EV'RYWHERE I GO
        I'VE PING AND PONG IN TOW.
        IF ONLY WE COULD TURN AND FLEE TO SOME LAND ACROSS THE SEAS
        WHERE I COULD SPEND TIME WITH MY FRIENDS
        WITHOUT THEM SHOUTING:

PING/PONG: FREEZE!

(*FSQ.3C; LXQ.6*)

ALL: ROUND AND ROUND THE PAGODAS,
        WATCHING THE WORLD GO BY –
        HIGH UP IN THE SKY
        BIRDIES GAILY FLY.
        ROUND AND ROUND THE PAGODAS,
        ALTHOUGH WE MAY BE POOR,
        WE WALK FOR HOURS
        AMONG THE FLOWERS
        AND NEVER ASK FOR MORE.
        EV'RYTHING IS LOVERLEY, LOVERLEY –
        EV'RYWHERE, EV'RYWHERE –
        MORNING, NOON AND NIGHT WE'RE ON THE GO –
        SO!
        ROUND AND ROUND THE PAGODAS, STROLLING EV'RYWHERE –
        WE LOVE IT WHEN THERE'S NOTHING TO DO WITH TIME TO STAND AND STARE.

(*LXQ.7; FSQ.3D*)

PING: Right, that's it, your Imperial Highness. You've had your fun. Now come along of us. Back to the Palace.

PONG: Yeh. A Princess cannot promenade round Pekin in the presence of a pauper.

JASMINE: Who says?

PONG: Your Pawpa – the Emperor.

PING: If your Imperial Dad knew the company you was keeping, he'd have us boiled in oil.

PONG: And served up as a fish supper.

ALADDIN: You always did have a chip on your shoulder.

PING: We'd better place this particular pauper under arrest.

(*PING and PONG produce huge notebooks and lick pencils.*)

PONG: Right! Aladdin, my lad, you're under a vest.

PING: Throw the book at him, Pong.

(*PONG throws his notebook at ALADDIN who ducks. It hits PING and knocks him over.*)

JASMINE: But you can't. He hasn't done anything. He's innocent.

PONG: Innocent? Ho ho ho.

PING: He's a feather-footed fly-by-night who gives a whole new meaning to "Chinese take-away."

PONG: Yeh. When he sees something Chinese – he takes it away.

JASMINE: But he's my hero. D'you know, I even dream about him.

PONG: Then I can only say, your Highness, as it must be somethin' you ate . . . heh heh . . .

(*LXQ.8; FSQ.4*)

Song: THE FIRST TIME I SAW YOU (*JASMINE and ALADDIN duet.*)

JASMINE: MY HEART WAS FANCY FREE;
AND LIFE MEANT NOTHING TO ME.
I THOUGHT THE FUTURE COULDN'T BE BRIGHT.

ALADDIN: BUT THEN YOU CAME MY WAY,
YOU TURNED MY NIGHT INTO DAY –

BOTH: IT MUST HAVE BEEN LOVE AT FIRST SIGHT.

THE FIRST TIME I SAW YOU, I KNEW AT A GLANCE,
I WAS MEANT TO BE YOURS – YOURS ALONE.
AS I STOOD BEFORE YOU, MY HEART SEEMED TO DANCE

AND I PRAYED YOU WOULD CALL ME YOUR OWN

WHEN I LOOK IN YOUR EYES,
I AM THRILLED TO THE SKIES
AND I FEEL LIKE A KING/QUEEN ON A THRONE

THE FIRST TIME I SAW YOU, I KNEW AT A GLANCE,
I WAS MEANT TO BE YOURS – YOURS ALONE.

(*During the duet, PING and PONG, elaborately furtive, try to manacle ALADDIN with their two pairs of manacles but, at the end of the song, ALADDIN runs off with JASMINE and WISHEE, leaving PING and PONG in a tangle of chains and handcuffed to each other.*)

(LXQ.9; FSQ.4A)

PING: Come ba . . . ! Oh! Foiled again.

(*PING and PONG are now hopelessly tangled back to back, hands between their legs and forced to shuffle as a pair.*)

PONG: (*Pointing truncheon*) Freeze!

PING: Don't be stupid. After him . . .

PONG: After her . . . !

(*They hop and shuffle off in pursuit. WISHEE WASHEE enters UL on the rostrum with a basket of washing.*)

WISHEE: (*Calling*) Washing done! Use Twankee's Laundry. Rinsing by royal appointment. Pressers to the palace. Our suds are superior. Our washing is wicked. Our creases are crucial . . . (*He trips down the steps, staggers and drops the washing DC.*) Oh look at that. I'll have to do it all again now. I work at Widow Twankee's Chinese Laundry. She says I'm stupid and idle. But I'm not really, am I?

AUDIENCE: Yes.

WISHEE: I'm not! I do the shopping and the mopping and the dripping and the drying 'til I drop. I cook the washing, put the dinner out and shove the cat through the mangle. No I don't. I put the washing out, shove the dinner through the mangle and cook the cat. No. Oh what do I do? (*With help from the AUDIENCE.*) That's it. I cook the *dinner*, put the *cat* out and shove the *washing* through the mangle. Then I water the garden and polish the gnome so I can't be that stupid. And then there's my gardening. Oh dear. (*He points to the plant.*) My Busy Lizzie looks a bit thirsty. This is my little plant. And she loves to be talked to. Don't oo 'ickle flower? Is ums alrightee?

(*The Flower squeaks.*) (**SQ.3**)

WISHEE: These are my friends.

(*The Flower looks out front and squeaks, impressed.*) (**SQ.4**)

WISHEE: Yes they *are* nice, aren't they? He likes you.

(*The Flower, overcome with shyness, squeaks coyly and hides its head.*) (**SQ.5**)

WISHEE: Actually, this is a magic plant. Every time I water it it'll grow a bit. You watch. (*He takes a watering can, waters flower and it grows a yard.*) It's good isn't it. I'm not really a very good gardener but I bred this myself. I crossed a fuschia with a dahlia. I call it a Failiah. You will keep an eye on it for me, won't you? Yeh. If anybody comes to touch it, I want you all to call out "SAVE THE FAILIAH" dead loud. Will you? I said will you? Here's somebody coming now. Let's give it a go.

(*Two PEKINESE enter furtively and approach the plant as if to steal it. The Failiah squeaks.*) (**SQ.6**)

AUDIENCE: Save the Failiah!

(*The PEKINESE scream and run off.*)

WISHEE: Massive! Ooops! Look out. Here comes Widow Twankee. She mustn't catch me with my flimsies on the floor. I'm off!

(*He gathers up his laundry and sprints off DR as WIDOW TWANKEE enters at speed DL, scooting on a very orientalised Supermarket Trolley.*)

(**LXQ.10; FSQ.5**)

TWANKEE: Hello, my dears. What a lovely looking lot you are. I hear we've got a trip from Brissle (*or wherever we are*) in town today. Is that right? I'm a Bedminster girl meself. Got

	shanghaied out shopping one Saturday and ended up in the street of a thousand hello sailors here in old Pekin. But you know, I'm terribly poor...
AUDIENCE:	Aaw...
TWANKEE:	Oh, I'm much poorer than that. I'm *really* poor...
AUDIENCE:	AAAWWW...
TWANKEE:	That's better. Yes. A poor widowed washerwoman left to bring up my rapscallion son, Aladdin, all alone. (*Sniffs.*) Are there some people from Clifton here? You can always tell. (*Seeing the Failiah and going towards it.*) Oh now that's a very pretty plant. I think I'll pick it and pot it for my patio...
AUDIENCE:	SAVE THE FAILIAH!
TWANKEE:	Alright, alright! (*To a member of the AUDIENCE.*) And what's your name? What? What? Abigail. I want everybody to say "Hello, Abigail." All together now... (*They do.*) There you are now, Abigail – it can't get more embarrassing after that. Lovely to see folk from home. I just want to shake you all by the hand. (*Shaking hands with the front row and any who can be reached.*) How d'you do? How d'you do? Charmed, I'm sure. The rest of you are a long way off, aren't you? Hang about a minute while I get me clothes prop. (*She brings on a very long pole with a gloved hand on the end and comes down into the auditorium with it.*) There now. (*Reaching up to the circle, boxes, gallery?*) How d'you do? How d'you do? Anybody want to kiss it, it's perfectly clean and soft thanks to Fairy Liquid. Ooo you've got cold hands, dear... No, shake it, dear, don't pick your nose with it. (*Back up onto the stage and gets rid of the prop.*) Now. Is anybody thirsty? Cup of tea? (*She throws out a teabag.*) Here's a good square meal... (*Oxo cube.*) Anybody fond of riding? (*Throws out toilet roll.*) There you are – Bronco. Crisps? Do you like the little ones? Here you are then... (*She flattens the bag.*) Oo look... (*Curtseying to the box.*) The Royals are in – Bert and Rita Royal from Redland... Bet you didn't know I'm a Spice Girl, did you? You've heard of Baby Spice and Ginger Spice? Well, I'm Old Spice – the smelly one. But I do know what I want... what I really really want...

(LXQ.11)

Dame Song: (*whatever is the current children's favourite*) – (*TWANKEE joined by the PEKINESE*)

(*Blackout.*) (*LXQ.12; FSQ.5A; FlyQ.2*) (*LXQ.13*)

Scene Two

A street in Pekin. ALADDIN and JASMINE enter furtively.

JASMINE: Aladdin . . . !

ALADDIN: It's alright. We've given them the slip.

JASMINE: But for how long? Oh, Aladdin . . . I can't stay. Ping and Pong are bound to catch me.

ALADDIN: Ping and Pong couldn't catch a cold. And we're alone at last – if only for a few minutes . . .

(*FSQ.6*)

Song: THE FIRST TIME I SAW YOU (Reprise)

(*During the dance, PING enters DL and PONG enters DR.*)

PING: (*Hoarse whisper*) There she is.

PONG: (*Hoarse whisper*) With him!

PONG: If the Emperor knew that she was dancing in the street with a washerwoman's son . . .

PING: He'd stretch us on the rack.

PONG: And that's the long and short of it.

PING: You hold onto *him* while I grab *her*.

PONG: Right.

(*PING grabs JASMINE and PONG grabs ALADDIN.*)

PING: Right! Come along, Princess . . .

PONG: Got her?

PING: Got her. Got him?

PONG: Got him.

PING: Right. H-e-a-ve.

(*ALADDIN and JASMINE are dragged slowly apart as they sing the last verse of their duet. But, on the coda, ALADDIN breaks free, rescues JASMINE and escapes with her. PING and PONG rush forward, collide and collapse in a heap.*)

(*Blackout.*)   (**LXQ.14;   FSQ.6A;   FlyQ.3**)   (**LXQ.15**)

Scene Three

Widow Twankee's Laundry. A door, UC with a sign above: WIDOW TWANKEE'S CHINESE LAUNDRY. A large front-loading washing machine with a glass door, L. A large mangle R. A washing line stretched across with a bench under it. WIDOW TWANKEE is C, possing washing in a tub amid clouds of bubbles.

TWANKEE: Oh hello, dears, I'm up to me armpits in it. Me hands is red raw. I do love it though – poshin' the washin' . . . It's better than a Bank Holiday in Birmingham. Times are hard though. No money about. 'S all this VAT – Very Ard Times. I nearly won the pools last week though. Me homes were alright – me aways were alright. But me drawers let me down. (*Holding up a very long pair of knickers.*)   All I want are some knickers like these – to keep me warm from me neck to me knees. (*Sings.*) "WE WILL – WE WILL – WASH YOU!" (*She holds up huge knickers.*) Pavarotti's a regular. (*Holds up tiny pair.*) And Ronnie Corbett. "WE WILL – WE WILL – WASH YOU!"

(*WISHEE WASHEE enters UC with a laundry basket.*)

WISHEE: Sorry I'm late, Widow Twankee, (*He bends to put the basket on the floor by the washing machine.*) I've got a little behind.

TWANKEE: I don't care what size it is you should've been here at nine o'clock.

WISHEE: Why? What happened then?

TWANKEE: (*She belts him with wet knickers*)   Now get to work.

WISHEE:	(*Picking up a large packet of soap powder from the top of the machine*) I think we're using the wrong stuff. Most people have given up Brand X.
	(*There is a loud, sinister knock at the door.*)
TWANKEE:	See who that is, Wishee Washee.
	(*WISHEE WASHEE goes to open the door. PING and PONG enter at speed, making police syren noises. PONG carries an armful of cones. PING has a flashing blue light on his helmet and carries a gong and beater. They circle the laundry and screech to a halt.*)
TWANKEE:	Oh it's Batman and Robin.
PING:	So . . . (*He takes out a bizarre identikit picture.*) You are Twankee, alias Widow?
TWANKEE:	I am.
PING:	You are a laundress of this city?
TWANKEE:	I am.
PING:	Weren't you Miss Cattarh of Cotham in 1953?
TWANKEE:	I was not.
PING:	You didn't say yes or no then, did you?
TWANKEE:	No . . . (*Gong.*) Ah!
PING:	Right, cone her off, Pong.
	(*PONG makes syren noises while he places traffic cones all round her.*)
TWANKEE:	(*Distressed*) Oh oh oh oh. What do you want, dears?
PING:	The . . . RENT!
TWANKEE:	(*Horrified*) The rent?
PING:	The . . . RENT! And if you don't pay us the . . . RENT! we're going to throw you out into the gutter.

Music: HEARTS AND FLOWERS

TWANKEE: (*On her knees*) Oh no! Oh, Ping! Oh Pong! Oh, Ping Pong! Not the gutter. I could never make my bread and butter in the gutter. Be merciful. Spare me. The quality of jerseys is not stained. By the power of St Michael's and Lord Littlewoods, spare this old scrubber.

PONG: Pardon?

TWANKEE: You heard. Spare this loveable laundress, this silver-haired old soak, this washworn weary old washer woman, I implore you. I appeal to you on my knees . . .

PONG: You don't appeal to me in any position.

TWANKEE: Oh please . . . (*Sobs.*) Please . . . (*Tears hair.*) Please . . . (*Bangs head on floor.*)

PING: I think she's after an Oscar.

PONG: It's not our fault, Widow Twankee. We're just obeying orders. We like you really. But we have to appear ugly.

WISHEE: That can't be very difficult.

(*PONG hits WISHEE with his truncheon.*)

PING: We have to appear tough and ruthless.

PONG: Yeh. Rough and toothless.

PING: (*Hitting PONG with his truncheon*) Shut up.

PONG: Sorry.

BOTH: Now. What about the . . . *RENT?*

TWANKEE: Well dears, I'm nearly there. I just need one more load of washing then I can pay. Just a minute. Pooh! You're a bit pongy, Ping and Pong, for policemen. A bit odiferous for officers. Rather rancid for rozzers . . .

PING: Alright, don't go on about it. But she's right. You're pretty dirty, Pong.

PONG: I'm even prettier when I'm clean.

TWANKEE: And so you shall be . . .

(LXQ.16; FSQ.7)

> *(TWANKEE and WISHEE sing a commercial while the TWANKEE sign flashes.)*
>
> TWANKEE'S. TWANKEE'S.
> WASH AT WIDOW TWANKEE'S.
> STAINS MAY COME
> BUT STAINS WILL GO
> AT WIDOW TWANKEE'S LAUNDRY –
> A PEE-ELL-CEEEEEE!

(LXQ.17; FSQ.7A)

TWANKEE: Tell you what. Special offer. Two for the price of one. But this offer ends in ten seconds' time. Ten – nine – eight . . .

(She leads the audience in a countdown while PING and PONG strip hurriedly to their long johns. WISHEE and TWANKEE are gathering up the clothes and throwing them into the washing machine. Finally, they throw in a pair of trousers which still has PONG inside them and slam the door.)

TWANKEE: Right, Wishee, my dear. Action stations.

(PONG'S worried face appears at the porthole of the washing machine.)

WISHEE: *(Springs to attention beside the machine)* Action stations.

TWANKEE: Load powder!

WISHEE: Load powder!

(WISHEE pours powder into the hatch at the top of the machine. It rains down onto PONG.)

TWANKEE: Close hatch!

WISHEE: *(Shutting the top hatch)* Close hatch!

TWANKEE: Set timer!

WISHEE: *(He turns a ratchet knob on the front of the machine)* Set timer!

ACT ONE

TWANKEE: Now . . . Throw the main switch.

WISHEE: (*Throwing a huge switch*) Throw the main switch!

(*There is an explosion (**SQ. 7**) and the machine lurches into life, belching bubbles. Clothes fly past the window with regular glimpses of PONG'S frantic face, sometimes upside down, sometimes going round, silently mouthing "HELP!!" TWANKEE and WISHEE sit down on stools in front of the machine and watch.*)

TWANKEE: Oh look! Brookside – the omnibus edition.

WISHEE: No it's Animal Hospital. Rolf'll come on in a minute.

(*The machine belches.*) (**SQ. 8**)

TWANKEE: Nothing but repeats.

(*During all this, PING has been searching for PONG, looking under the cones, in the washing baskets, in the tub, etc. The machine stops with a bang. (**SQ. 9**) The door flies open and a very small policeman, face completely hidden under the helmet and jacket reaching to the floor, falls out.*)

PING: Pong! PONG! What have they done to you, Pong?

PONG: (*Very high pitched*) Hello hello hello.

TWANKEE: Never mind, dear. Stick him in a growbag and he'll come up a treat.

(*PING exits, leading the tiny PONG to "Laurel and Hardy" theme.*)

WISHEE: Well that's dealt with that, Widow Twankee.

TWANKEE: Yes. Now let's get this washing hung out.

(*They start to hang out washing on the line. There is a loud, slow, sinister knock at the door.*)

WISHEE: Look out.

TWANKEE: Oh no. They're not back again. Quick. Peg yourself out.

(They stand on the bench under the washing line and pretend to be washing. The knock is repeated.)

TWANKEE: Come in if you're pretty.

(The door creaks open. (SQ.10) ABANAZAR enters.)

TWANKEE: It's Michael Portillo!

ABANAZAR: *(Looking round)* Nobody here. Very well, *(Producing a large snuffbox.)* I'll take a sniff of my favourite snuff while I wait. *(He sits on the bench between them, opens the snuff box and takes a huge pinch of snuff, scattering it liberally into the air. After a series of facial contortions, all three sneeze at once.)*

ABANAZAR: *(Seeing TWANKEE)* Ah. Madam. What are you doing there?

TWANKEE: Just hanging about, dear.

ABANAZAR: *(Helping her down, kissing her hand and getting a clothes peg stuck in his mouth)* Greetings, my good woman.

TWANKEE: *(Stepping down)* Who's been talking?

ABANAZAR: Are not you the widow of the late lamented Hoo Flung Twankee?

TWANKEE: *(Instantly dramatic)* Yes. *(With a sob, getting out hanky.)* I am she. *(She blows her nose, long and loud, on her hanky and wrings it out.)*

ABANAZAR: Then come – *(Doing so.)* let me crush you to my bosom, woman of my dreams.

TWANKEE: Never mind about crushing *your* bosom, *(Re-arranging her bust.)* you're knocking mine all over the shop.

ABANAZAR: Dear Mrs Twankee, I have travelled from the desolate desert of the Sahara to bring you the warmth, the wealth and the welcome of a loving brother-in-law.

TWANKEE: The wealth?

ABANAZAR: Beyond your wildest dreams.

ACT ONE

TWANKEE: I have some pretty wild dreams. But, just a minute – the late Mr Twankee never said anything about a brother.

ABANAZAR: Ah. Poor Hoo Flung. He was too ashamed to mention me. You see, as he grew poorer, I, Abanazar, grew richer. Everything I touched turned to gold . . .

TWANKEE: That must have been tricky . . .

ABANAZAR: . . . until now I'm so rich that money means nothing to me.

TWANKEE: It doesn't mean a lot to me either.

ABANAZAR: But I lack the love of a wonderful, well-built woman and a strapping nephew to call me Uncle. By the way? Where is Aladdin?

TWANKEE: Aladdin? You're too late.

ABANAZAR: Too late? (*Fearing the worst.*) Oh NO! He's not . . . dead? Ah no no no no NO!

TWANKEE: (*Cradling his head and patting him*) There there there. He's not dead.

ABANAZAR: He's not?

TWANKEE: No. He's a bit slow maybe. But he's not dead.

ABANAZAR: I have good news for him.

TWANKEE: Oh really? How good?

ABANAZAR: There's a fortune in it.

TWANKEE: That's good. Wishee Washee, go and get Aladdin. He's in the kitchen mending the broken biscuits.

(*WISHEE goes off DR.*)

ABANAZAR: I require Aladdin to aid me in the recovery of . . . something I require. If Aladdin helps me to acquire what I desire, you will never again need to worry about your arears.

TWANKEE: (*Looking behind her*) Pardon?

ABANAZAR: Whatever you want will be yours.

TWANKEE: I'll have a pint of Philosan please.

ALADDIN: (*Entering with WISHEE*) What is it, Mother?

TWANKEE: Aladdin, I want you to meet your long lost uncle – Avabanana.

ABANAZAR: Abanazar.

TWANKEE: He wants you to get him something.

ABANAZAR: (*He grips ALADDIN'S hand*) Aladdin! (*He punches ALADDIN'S shoulder.*) Dear nephew . . . !

ALADDIN: Uncle! (*He punches ABANAZAR'S shoulder.*)

ABANAZAR: (*Reeling and clutching his shoulder*) Dear lad . . . I want you to come with me, Aladdin, to retrieve a long lost treasure hidden in a cave in the mountains of . . . (*High pitched.*) Howwaannghawawahaaah . . .

ALADDIN: Howaangh . . . ?

ABANAZAR: . . . awawahaah.

TWANKEE: He means the Mendips.

ABANAZAR: It was a mission, Aladdin, which poor Hoo Flung, your father, never completed. He was waylaid by bandits and murdered. It's up to you now. The rewards are great.

ALADDIN: Oh mother, to avenge my father and to find my own fortune. To be rich. Who knows, maybe I could marry the Princess.

TWANKEE: And maybe I can get married. What do you think, Ali Baba?

ABANAZAR: (*Crossly*) Abanazar. (*To ALADDIN.*) But see – the sun sets. We must depart. Will you come?

ALADDIN: Out of respect for my father, of course I'll come. Goodbye, Mother. I must go and get ready.

TWANKEE: (*Tearfully*) But, my little boy . . . Aladdin. What if there's . . . danger?

ABANAZAR: I will take care of him, my dear, have no fear.

TWANKEE: You're a good uncle, Abercrombie.

ABANAZAR: (*Quietly furious*) Abanazar! (*Aside, laughing.*) Poor fools! Little do they know ...
That, once the lamp is mine to rub,
I'll beat his brains out with a club
Or else imprison him in the cave – a fine place to go mad in.
And, bye and bye,
He will starve and die.
Come. Walk this way, Aladdin!

(*He exits UC sniggering nastily with ALADDIN trying to copy his "villain's" walk.*)

TWANKEE: (*Weeping and wailing*) Oh, Aladdin! My little boy! My only son and hairpiece! What will I do without him? What will I ...? (*Suddenly normal.*) Right come on, Wishee Washee, we've just time to put this washing through the mangle before we go to see him off.

WISHEE: Righto, Widow T.

TWANKEE: Now, when we do the mangling, what must you do?

WISHEE: (*Childish*) I must mind my fingers.

TWANKEE: Mind your fingers. What must he do, boys and girls?

AUDIENCE: Mind his fingers!

TWANKEE: (*Limbering at the handle*) Right. Mind your fingers. Here we go then.

(*WISHEE picks up a pink sock from the basket and takes it to the mangle.*)

TWANKEE: What must he do?

AUDIENCE: Mind his fingers!

TWANKEE: Right.

(*She turns the handle, ratchet noise from the pit, the sock disappears. She turns the handle back and out comes a huge stiff flat pink sock.*)

TWANKEE: See what I mean? Next.

WISHEE: (*Bringing a nightshirt*) Here we are ...

TWANKEE: Ah-ah! What must he do?

AUDIENCE: Mind his fingers . . .

WISHEE: Mind my fingers . . . Alright, alright, I know!

(*The nightshirt goes through but doesn't come back.*)

TWANKEE: Oh well. (*Sings.*) Another one bites the dust. Next.

WISHEE: (*With a boilersuit*) This is next . . .

TWANKEE: And what must he do?

AUDIENCE: Mind his fingers . . .

WISHEE: (*Crossly to the AUDIENCE, not minding his fingers – TWANKEE is winding steadily, not looking at him.*) Alright. Alright. I am minding my . . . Oooooohhhh . . . !

(*He is drawn in between the rollers and vanishes into the mangle. TWANKEE stops winding and looks round for him.*)

TWANKEE: Where did he go? Where did Wishee go? Where?

AUDIENCE: In the mangle!

TWANKEE: In the mangle? Oh no . . .

(*She starts to reverse the mangle, slowly winding out a very flat* (cutout) *WISHEE WASHEE who drops to the floor. She picks him up.*)

TWANKEE: Oh, Wishee. My poor Wishee. (*She folds him over her arm.*) Looks like he had a pressing engagement.

(*Blackout.*)   (*LXQ.18; FlyQ.4*)   (*LXQ.19*)

Scene Four

A Street in Old Pekin. A BABY CAMEL enters DL and crosses the stage. She sees the flower and goes towards it, as if to eat it.

AUDIENCE: Save the failiah!

(*The CAMEL panics and runs off DR. PING and PONG enter DL.*)

PONG: (*Holding his truncheon like a gun*) Freeze! Nobody move. The place is surrounded.

PING: Don't be daft. There's nobody here.

PONG: Oh (*The truncheon droops.*) Well, I'll tell you one thing, Ping – we won't be seeing Aladdin anymore. Not once he's gone to the Mountains of Howaang . . .

PING: . . . awawaahaaaaah?

PONG: Nobody *ever* comes back from there.

PING: Oh I dunno. I often go up there – to watch the pandas.

PONG: That's a long way to walk to watch pandas.

PING: I always go in the panda car.

(*PONG pushes a piece of string into his ear and (apparently) pulls it out of the other.*)

PING: What's that?

PONG: Mental floss.

(*Enter ALADDIN, JASMINE, WISHEE WASHEE, ABANAZAR, the PEKINESE and the CAMEL DR. The PEKINESE are weeping.*)

JASMINE: Oh, Aladdin, I shall miss you . . .

(*TWANKEE, in full mountaineering gear, with packs and everything – including the kitchen sink – enters DR to "THE HAPPY WANDERER". She is sobbing loudly.*)

ABANAZAR: Never fear, dear Mrs Twankee, he'll be safe in my hands. Here, lovely lady, (*Drawing his dagger.*) let me cut you a flower . . . (*He goes to the plant.*)

AUDIENCE: Save the Failiah!

ABANAZAR: (*To the AUDIENCE*) How I hate interfering busybodies! (*He spits into the flower pot. The Failiah grows. He reacts.*) And now we must be on our way.

ALADDIN: Goodbye, Princess. Goodbye, Mother. Goodbye, everybody.

(*LXQ.20; FSQ.8*)

        Song: WISH ME LUCK (*ALADDIN and CHORUS*)

ALADDIN: WISH ME LUCK AS YOU WAVE ME GOODBYE –
CHEERIO. HERE I GO – ON MY WAY.

WISHEE: IF YOU LEAVE US TO GRIEVE, WE WILL CRY
AND BE GLUM – 'TIL YOU COME – BACK TO STAY.

ABANAZAR: LET'S BE GONE SOON
ERE THE SUN TURNS TO MOON
AND THE DARKNESS ENDS THE DAY.

PING: HIT THE TRACK!

PONG: DON'T COME BACK!

BOTH: BYESIE-BYE!

ALL: WE WISH YOU LUCK AS WE WAVE YOU GOODBYE.

JASMINE: THOUGH TO PART BREAKS MY HEART AND I DIE,
IN MY TOW'R, HOUR BY HOUR, I WILL WAIT.
WHILE MY FEARS MAY BRING TEARS TO MY EYE –

PING: THIS IS IT!

ABANAZAR: TIME TO SPLIT!

PONG: SHUT THE GATE!

JASMINE: I WILL GIVE YOU A SMILE
YOU CAN KEEP ALL THE WHILE
IN YOUR HEART WHILE YOU'RE AWAY.

ALL: 'TIL WE MEET IN THE SWEET BYE AND BYE,
WE WISH YOU LUCK AS WE WAVE YOU GOODBYE.

ALADDIN: DISDAINING ALL DANGER, I'LL TRY
FOR THE POOR TO BRING FORTUNE AND WEALTH.

TWANKEE: JUST BE SURE TO KEEP YOUR TOOTSIES DRY.
FOR YOUR DAD, IT WAS BAD FOR HIS HEALTH.

ABANAZAR: BUT ENOUGH OF THIS SONG!
WE SHOULD HURRY ALONG.

FOR THE LAST BUS WE MUST FLY!

ALL: 'TIL WE MEET IN THE SWEET BYE AND BYE –
WE WISH YOU LUCK AS WE WAVE YOU – GOODBYE!

(*ABANAZAR pulls ALADDIN off DL.*)

(*LXQ.21; FSQ.8A*)

(*All exit singing and waving goodbye except the JASMINE and the CAMEL, left alone and weeping. The CAMEL nuzzles up to her and they make a sad exit DR. Blackout.*)

(*LXQ.22; FSQ.8B; FlyQ.5*) (*LXQ.23*)

Scene Five

The Mountains of Howaangawawahaa. Sinister Music. Smoke. Cawing of rooks, wind, rumbling thunder. (**SQ.11**) *ALADDIN and ABANAZAR* (apparently) *hack their way on through dense foliage.*

ALADDIN: We have come a wild and weary way, Uncle Abanazar. Through alligator-infested swamps and jungles filled with savage beasts. Is there much further to go?

ABANAZAR: Why no, lad, we are here. This is our destination.

ALADDIN: (*Looking out front*) But this is a bleak and fearful wasteland, Uncle, desolate and dreadful and without hope.

ABANAZAR: Aye, Cannons Marsh (*local eyesore*) they call this, lad. But fear nothing for I am here. You're safe enough with me and we are now within an ace of making your fortune.

ALADDIN: I see no sign of riches here . . .

ABANAZAR: (*Turning and pointing*) Up yonder. See. We have but to scale this cliff before us to find the entrance to the cave wherein your fortune lies. You're not afraid, are you?

ALADDIN: Of course not, Uncle.

ABANAZAR: No. You're a plucky lad. I'll see no harm comes to you. You do trust me, don't you?

ALADDIN: Of course, Uncle.

ABANAZAR: (*Aside*) Then the more fool you . . . Heh heh heh . . .

AUDIENCE: HISS.

ALADDIN: What's that noise? That hissing sound?

ABANAZAR: (*Trying to hush the kids*) Snakes.

ALADDIN: It's too loud for snakes.

ABANAZAR: 'Tis naught but the wind in the willows. Aye, 'tis the hurricane howling through the bare branches of the blasted trees – like so many blasted KIDS! (*Leading him to the foot of the mountain.*) Here, lad . . . Here is the way. Climb up. Climb up.

ALADDIN: (*To the AUDIENCE*) Should I, I wonder?

AUDIENCE: No . . . !

ALADDIN: It's as though I could hear voices warning me to turn back, Uncle . . .

ABANAZAR: No no. Just an abominable snowman jogging past with his walkman on too loud. Climb up, lad and give me a hand . .

ALADDIN: (*Climbing*) Of course, Uncle. Here take my hand . . .

ABANAZAR: Thank you, lad . . . (*Struggling up.*) You're very kind to your poor old uncle.

ALADDIN: Not much further. There seems to be a ledge up here. There now. Rest awhile.

ABANAZAR: Ah. Thank you, lad. (*As if amazed.*) Why – bless me! This is the very spot. This is the way into the mountain.

ALADDIN: There's nothing here but solid rock.

ABANAZAR: That's because you have yet to speak the spell.

ALADDIN: Speak the spell?

ABANAZAR: (*Whispers*) Open Sesame.

ALADDIN: (*Aloud*) Open Sesame?

ACT ONE

          (*There is a crack of thunder (**SQ.12;**   **LXQ.24**) and the cliff shakes.*)

ABANAZAR: (*In panic*) Not yet! These things must be done right or they go *horribly* wrong. First you must turn round three times.

ALADDIN: (*Turning precariously on the ledge*) Like this?

ABANAZAR: One. Two. Three. Now strike the rock three times with your hand . . .

ALADDIN: Like this? (*striking the rock – tymp. in pit.*)

ABANAZAR: One. Two. Three. Now. (*Holding on to the rock and shutting his eyes.*) Speak the spell.

ALADDIN: Open Sesame!

          (*A deafening clap of thunder. (**SQ.13;**   **LXQ.25**) Immediate night. (**LXQ.26**) Flashes of lightning, a howling wind and more thunder as the cliff begins to move, revolving slowly . . .*)

TRANSFORMATION MUSIC.

ALADDIN: (*Shouting above the noise*) What's happening? It must be an earthquake . . . or an avalanche. Stay close to me Uncle, I'll not let you fall. Hold on . . .

(**LXQ.27**)

ABANAZAR: I'm holding on . . .

ALADDIN: The whole mountain seems to be moving . . .

          (*The cave door pivots open as the cliff revolves and the scene transforms into:*)

(**LXQ.28**)

Scene Six

The Cavern of the Wonderful Lamp. ALADDIN and ABANAZAR are now upstage gazing down into the cavern which glitters with jewels. The lamp, old and battered and dusty, stands on a plinth.

ALADDIN: Why... Uncle... I never saw the like. See. There are chests of gold, great jars of emeralds, amethysts and diamonds, trees of silver and gold with sapphires and rubies growing on them...

ABANAZAR: Aye. And see yonder... A dusty lamp waiting to be rubbed clean...

ALADDIN: There must be a fortune here. A king's ransome...

ABANAZAR: Aye. And a dusty lamp waiting to be rubbed clean...

ALADDIN: I never saw such riches...

ABANAZAR: Aye. They dazzle you lad, do they not. Go in. Enter. Climb down and fill your pockets...

(LXQ.29)

ALADDIN: (*Climbing down into the cavern*) Just wait 'til I carry all these home. Mother's waited all her life for riches like these.

ABANAZAR: (*Aside*) And she'll wait a good while longer... (*Aloud.*) Fill up your pockets, lad. And fill up those bags. Bring all you can carry for now and we'll return for the rest another day...

ALADDIN: (*Filling his pockets*) Why, I'll be the richest man in Pekin. Richer than the Emperor. I'll be able to go to him and ask for Princess Jasmine's hand in marriage... (*Shovelling jewels into the bags.*) Why don't you come in, Uncle, and help yourself?

ABANAZAR: Aye. I should like that but... (*He moves to enter the cavern. There is an ominous rumbling.* **(SQ14)** *He starts back.*) No. It's too much for an old man, lad. I'll just sit here and watch you...

ALADDIN: Then I shall bring jewels for you, too.

ABANAZAR: Nay, lad. All I require is a trinket. Let me see...That lamp now. Aye. That takes my fancy. Something to remind me of our little expedition together. Fetch me that lamp for me to treasure as a keepsake...

ALADDIN: (*Picking up the lamp*) What? This old thing? It's battered and filthy. Here, I'll give it a clean before I fetch it to you.

ABANAZAR: (*Panic*) DON'T RUB IT!!

ALADDIN: What?

ABANAZAR: Fetch it just as it is. Come on, lad. Fetch it to me . . .

ALADDIN: (*Struggling to climb back up*) It's hard with these bags on my shoulder. These jewels are heavy.

ABANAZAR: (*Reaching down to him*) Come on, lad. Come on . . .

ALADDIN: I'm trying, Uncle . . .

ABANAZAR: You certainly are. Give me the lamp to lighten your load.

ALADDIN: Reach down further and give me your hand . . .

ABANAZAR: Give me the lamp.

ALADDIN: Give me your hand and then I can give you the lamp.

ABANAZAR: Give me the lamp and then I'll give you my hand.

ALADDIN: Uncle, please. Give me your hand.

ABANAZAR: (*Furious*) Give me the lamp, blast you! Give me the lamp!

ALADDIN: What's so important about this old lamp?

ABANAZAR: Nothing. Nothing. Give it to me. Do as I say.

ALADDIN: Should I?

AUDIENCE: No.

ALADDIN: There are those voices again, Uncle. They seem to be warning me of something.

ABANAZAR: They should learn to MIND THEIR OWN BUSINESS!!

ALADDIN: I don't think you're being honest with me, Uncle.

ABANAZAR: Not honest? Moi?

ALADDIN: I don't think you've told me the real reason for our coming here. And, until you do, I'm not moving from this place.

ABANAZAR: Ah! Curses! Curses! Stupid boy! Give me that lamp or I'll lock you in and leave you to starve.

ALADDIN: But, Uncle . . . !

ABANAZAR: Uncle? I'm not your uncle. You have no uncle – you were too poor. I am the bandit that put an end to your father but had no means to get at his fortune – the lamp! But soon you'll give it to me willingly. Aye. By the time I return, you'll give me anything I want for a crust of bread. For now, farewell. (*He strikes the rock three times.*) "Close Sesame!" Ha ha haaaa!

(*There is a crack of thunder* (*SQ.15*) *and the cave entrance closes.*) (*LXQ.30*)

ALADDIN: All these riches now are naught but a cruel joke. There's no escape from here. I shall starve to death and never see the Princess again . . .

(*LXQ.31; FSQ.9*)

Song: LOVE IS EVERYWHERE (*Trio*) (*ALADDIN, PRINCESS and THYLVIA*)

ALADDIN: EVEN IN THIS DREADFUL PLACE
STILL I SEE YOUR LOVELY FACE
EVER DEAR –
AND SEEMING EVER NEAR
TURNING FEAR TO LAUGHTER.

(*LXQ.32*) (*JASMINE, "dreamlike" appears behind a gauze in the rock.*)

JASMINE: NOW, TO ME, IT REALLY SEEMS
YOU'RE THE ANSWER TO MY DREAMS . . .

BOTH: WE HAVE FOUND THE WAY TO PARADISE
FOR EVER AFTER . . .

(*LXQ.33*) (*THYLVIA appears behind a gauze in another part of the rock.*

A & J: LOVE IS EV'RYWHERE   THYLVIA: WUB YOUR WING!
LIKE A MELODY WITHOUT   GIVE YOUR WING A
                                          WUB!
AN ENDING –
TO ITS STRAINS A MILLION   IN A FLATH

HEARTS ARE BENDING, LOVE IS EV'RYWHERE. LOVE IS EV'RYWHERE	I WILL DATH PLEASE WUB YOUR WING
IN THE MAGIC MYSTERY OF MOONLIGHT IN THE HAUNTING SPLEN- DOURS OF A JUNE NIGHT	THEN WE'LL BATH THAT TWATH ABANATHAR AND THAVE YOU TOO.
BY A STROKE OF CHANCE OUR HEARTS HAVE FOUND ROMANCE WE'LL DO OUR BEST TO MAKE IT STAY AND ALL OUR LIFETIME THROUGH OUR LOVE WILL STILL BE TRUE WHATEVER FATE MAY SEND OUR WAY.	WUB IT! WUB IT! NOW! WUB IT! WUB IT! NOW!
LOVE IS EV'RYWHERE IN THE WORDS THESE LIPS OF MINE ARE SINGING EVEN IN THE DREAMS THE NIGHT IS BRINGING LOVE IS EV'RYWHERE LOVE IS EV'RYWHERE.	WUB YOUR WING! GIVE YOUR WING A WUB! WUB YOUR WING NOW, ALADDIN! AND YOU WILL THEE... I CAN THET YOU FWEE!

(*JASMINE and THYLVIA fade and ALADDIN is alone again.*) (**LXQ.34; FSQ.9A**)

ALADDIN: Why, here's a golden ring with a sapphire in it. But how can a ring help me to escape?

(*A sign appears round the proscenium saying: "WUB IT".*)

AUDIENCE: Wub it.

ALADDIN: Wub it? Wub the wing? I mean rub the ring? But what good would that do? Oh well, I'll try anything just at the moment. (*He rubs the ring.*) There...

(*A Flash.* (**LXQ.35; PyroQ.3**) *THYLVIA appears.*)

ALADDIN: Who are you?

THYLVIA:	I am Thylvia, Thlave of the Wing.
ALADDIN:	I beg your pardon?
THYLVIA:	Thylvia. Thlave of the Wing.
ALADDIN:	Oh Sylvia, Slave of the Ring.
THYLVIA:	That'th what I thaid.
ALADDIN:	Of course it is.
THYLVIA:	I am thent to therve you and thave you fwom thith thinithter plathe.
ALADDIN:	How can you do that?
THYLVIA:	By twanthporting you back to Pekin.
ALADDIN:	Twanthporting? I mean transporting?
THYLVIA:	That'th what I thaid. I'm vewy good at twanthportathion thpellth. (*She produces a pocket calculator and moves ALADDIN further L, turning him round.*)
ALADDIN:	What are you doing now?
THYLVIA:	Jutht thetting the co-ordinateth. There now. (*Producing her wand and incanting.*) Thummon tempethtth and thtormth and a fwiendly bweethe To cawwy Aladdin above the tweeth. Acwoth fowetht and thwamp and plathe him down Thafely in hith native town. (*There is a Flash (**LXQ.36; PyroQ.4**) and ALADDIN disappears.*)
THYLVIA:	There now. That thould thee him thafely back to Pekin. But whereaboutth in Pekin – well that'th a diffewent kettle of fith altogether. If only I could join the Magic Thircle and learn to do thpellth pwoperly.

(*LXQ.37; FSQ.10*)

Song: THYLVIA'TH THONG (*THYLVIA*)

THYLVIA:	I HAVE GOT A PWOBLEM – JUTHT A TINY THNAG –

I CAN'T PWONOUNTHE MY ETHETH –
IT'TH WEALLY THUTCH A DWAG.
FOLKTH MITHUNDERTHTAND ME
UNLETH I WRITE IT DOWN.
LIKE WHEN I THAID "I'M THINKING"
I MEANT THAT I WOULD DWOWN!
THUCH A THILLY PWOBLEM –
MAKETH ME THO DEPWETHED –
TO FIND A BWILL THOLUTHION
ITH MY LIFE-LONG QUETHT.
PEOPLE MOCK THE WAY I THPEAK
IT MAKETH MY LIFE A HELL.
LIKE WHEN I THAID "I'M WATHER THICK"
I MEANT I DON'T FEEL WELL.
WHAT A HOWID PWOBLEM –
BUT THERE'TH WORTH FOR ME.
I CAN'T ETHCAPE THE WING
'TIL I THPEAK THE THPELL TO THET ME FWEE
BUT, TWY ATH I MIGHT,
I CANNOT QUITE
MY ATHOTHITHION THEVER.
THE THPELL ITH "ITHY WITHY"
THO I THINK I'M THTUCK FOR EVER!

(*Blackout.*) (**LXQ.38; FSQ.10A; FlyQ.6**)   (**LXQ.39**)

Scene Seven

A Street in Pekin. JASMINE enters with WISHEE, PING, PONG and the PEKINESE. All are weeping.

PEKE: Oh ... Where's Aladdin, Princess?

PEKE: Why's he gone so long?

JASMINE: Oh I don't know, children. We've not heard a word from him – no text messages – not even a fax. I only hope nothing awful has happened to him.

PEKE: Perhaps he's been eaten by a panda.

JASMINE: (*Seeing their distress*) I'm sure he'll be alright. He's able to take care of himself. (*They are not convinced.*) Do you know what I do when I feel worried? I sing a little song.

WISHEE: Oh, I know a song. I sing it daily. That's why I've brought ... (*Producing it.*) My ukelele!

(*LXQ.40; FSQ.11*)

        Song: HAPPINESS PIE (*WISHEE, PRINCESS, PING, PONG and CHORUS*)

WISHEE: SMILING IS THE LATEST THING IN STYLE,
SO CHEER UP AND WEAR A BIG BROAD SMILE.
IF YOU WANT TO BE HAPPY,
LISTEN CLOSELY TO ME –
IF YOU WANT TO BE HAPPY,
FOLLOW THIS RECIPE:

(*LXQ.41; FSQ.11A*)

ALL: TAKE A CUP AND A HALF OF SUNBEAMS,
POUR THEM INTO A DEEP BLUE SKY,
ADD A COUPLE OF DROPS OF LOVE DREAMS,
AND MAKE YOURSELF A HAPPINESS PIE.
TAKE A SPOONFUL OF PLEASANT WEATHER,
ANY JUNE DAY WILL QUALIFY,
STIR THE MIXTURE ALL UP TOGETHER
AND MAKE YOURSELF A HAPPINESS PIE!
REMEMBER FOUR AND TWENTY BLACKBIRDS
ONE DAY WERE BAKED INTO A PIE
BUT JUST FORGET ABOUT THE BLACKBIRDS
WITH THE BLUEBIRDS SO CLOSE BY.
HAVE A FILLING OF HUGS AND KISSES
WITH A SWEETNESS TO SATISFY,
FOR YOU DON'T KNOW WHAT LOVE AND BLISS IS
'TIL YOU MAKE YOURSELF A HAPPINESS PIE!

(*FSQ.11B*)

    (*They end in a wild, noisily joyful dance. It dies away as WIDOW TWANKEE enters tragically.*)

(*LXQ.42; FSQ.11C*)

TWANKEE: Do you mind? Do you flipping mind? What's all this kerfuffle then? Like a Saturday at Asda's when they've a special offer on. Can't you see I'm upset? Can't you show some respect for my melancholia? Please! Be so kind as to belt up!

WISHEE: But, Widow Twankee. It's terrible. Aladdin's missing and we're all heartbroken.

TWANKEE: We must look on the bright side. We must tell ourselves that, any minute now, he'll come round that corner with his fortune made and rich as Richard Branson. Then we'll be able to afford a cup of tea in Dingles.

ALL: Hooray.

TWANKEE: We could have a day out at Toys 'R' Us.

ALL: Hooray.

TWANKEE: We could even get a season ticket for the (*local football team*).

ALL: Eaugh.

PEKE: (*Bursting into tears*) I want Aladdin . . .

(*PONG bursts into tears joined by all the other children and WISHEE WASHEE.*)

JASMINE: Oh please cheer up. Come on, children, let's get you back home. It's time for bed.

(*JASMINE, PING and the PEKINESE exit sadly DR and DL. PONG remains, standing next to TWANKEE, crying bitterly.*)

TWANKEE: Oh pong yourself together, Pull. I mean pull yourself together, Pong. You're a big boy now. Go and see if you can find him.

PONG: Righto.

TWANKEE: Well go on then.

PONG: Righto.

TWANKEE: Why do you keep saying righto?

PONG: You're standing on my right toe.

(*She lifts her foot and he hops off.*)

TWANKEE: Wishee Washee, we've got to do something to cheer ourselves up.

WISHEE: Nothing can cheer me up. I'm feeling really flat.

TWANKEE: We must keep ourselves busy. I know that Aladdin will come home and when he does he'll be hungry. And it'll be his birthday. So. What we're going to do is to bake him . . . a *Birthday Cake!!* (*To the AUDIENCE.*) Oh yes we are . . .

WISHEE: Good idea.

TWANKEE: Walk this way . . . Oh no, that lovely Uncle Abanazar's already done that one . . .

(*The front cloth flies out* (***FlyQ.7;   LXQ.43***) *to reveal:*)

Scene Eight

WIDOW TWANKEE'S Kitchen. There is a large Table C with a cloth reaching to the floor (*to mask all the props stacked underneath*). *A huge Welsh Dresser stands UL. This is double-sided and revolves so that the JINI* (*and later JASMINE*) *can be transported round on it at speed. A large Cooker stands UR.*

TWANKEE: (*Taking her Apron from a peg on the Welsh Dresser and putting it on*) Now then. We must be ready for the rover's return. (*To the AUDIENCE.*) I have missed him. He's so clever. He got a first at Oxford, a second at Cambridge, and a the third in the four thirty at Chepstow. I'm fond of Wishee Washee too, you know. He grew up with Aladdin. They wore the same size in nappies – two and a half litres.

(*WISHEE stops to water the FALIAH. It grows.*)

TWANKEE: Wishee Washee!

WISHEE: Here, Widow Twankee.

TWANKEE: Do you like my recipe apron?

WISHEE: Your recipe apron?

TWANKEE: Yes. Look. (*Unvelcroes a flap revealing a large slice of bread.*) Bread and butter pudding . . . And here . . . (*Second flap, giant fish-fingers.*) Fish fingers . . . And here . . . (*Drops bib to reveal a raincoat.*) Big Mac . . . (*Turns round.*) And for afters. (*She drops the flap on her bottom which shows an elaborate ice cream sundae.*) Knickerbocker Glory. ' Course, my cooking should be cordon bleu.

ACT ONE

WISHEE: You cooking should be cordoned off. (*He takes off his hat – with pigtail attached – and takes his Chef's hat – with another pigtail attached – and puts it on.*)

TWANKEE: Cheek! Let's get on with this cake then.

WISHEE: Very well. Have you got the ingredients.

TWANKEE: A bit, dear. I shouldn't have eaten all those beans. (*She takes a big book from the table and blows dust off.*) Now first of all we need a bowl. Get the bowl. Get it?

WISHEE: (*Bringing bowl from under the table*) Got it.

TWANKEE: Good. First, we need some nuts. Get 'em?

WISHEE: (*Producing a tin of steel nuts*) Got 'em.

TWANKEE: Good. Tip 'em in.

(*WISHEE WASHEE tips the steel nuts into the bowl.*)

TWANKEE: Now some oil.

(*WISHEE produces a giant oil can and squirts oil into the bowl.*)

TWANKEE: A soupçon more?

(*Another squirt. TWANKEE dips in her finger and licks it.*)

TWANKEE: Mmm. Supergreen. Now we need some flour. Get it?

WISHEE: (*Producing a plastic flower*) Got it.

TWANKEE: Good.

(*WISHEE puts it in.*)

TWANKEE: (*Taking it out*) No not a flow-er F-L-O-W-E-R but (*Making the sounds.*) FUH-LUH-O-U-RUH. Huh?

WISHEE: FUH – LUH – O – U – RUH, HUH?

TWANKEE: FUH – LUH – O – U – RUH, HUH?

WISHEE: Oh . . . ! FUH – LUH – O – U – RUH, HUH!

TWANKEE: Yes! FUH – LUH – O – U – RUH, HUH.

(They repeat, becoming rhythmic, with increasing percussion accompaniment from the pit, ending up in a rhumba routine, WISHEE with the flower in his mouth.)

TWANKEE: Will you stop it. Now get it.

WISHEE: *(Producing a huge flour shaker)* Got it.

TWANKEE: Good. Now sprinkle on the flour.

(The flour shaker rises slowly up in the air, taking WISHEE'S arm.)

TWANKEE: What are you doing?

WISHEE: It's self-raising.

TWANKEE: No no no. You sprinkle it from a height.

(WISHEE climbs up on the table and sprinkles it from a height. All over WIDOW TWANKEE.)

TWANKEE: Alright. Alright. That's plenty. Can't tell which is flour and which is dandruff. Now we need some water for the dough. Get it?

WISHEE: *(Produces a water pistol)* Got it.

TWANKEE: Good. Give it to me.

(WISHEE squirts TWANKEE.)

TWANKEE: Not in my face. In the bowl!

WISHEE: Oh . . . *(He squirts into the bowl.)*

TWANKEE: Now we need three eggs. Get 'em?

WISHEE: *(Produces box of eggs)* Got 'em.

TWANKEE: Good. Put them in the bowl.

WISHEE: Oh. I know a little trick with an egg, Widow T.

TWANKEE: A little trick?

WISHEE: With an egg. Can I show you?

TWANKEE: If you must.

WISHEE: (*Doing so*) I take one egg . . .

TWANKEE: One egg . . .

WISHEE: (*Doing so*) I take one plate . . .

TWANKEE: One plate . . .

WISHEE: I throw the egg high up in the air . . .

(*He does so. Drumroll.*)

WISHEE: . . . and I catch it . . . on the plate . . . without breaking it!

(*He does – without breaking it. A triumphant chord. This takes a bit of practice but the trick is to slip the plate under the egg while it is still in the air and move down with it, "braking' gently.*)

TWANKEE: I can do that.

WISHEE: Oh no you can't.

TWANKEE: Oh yes I can.

WISHEE: Oh no you can't.

TWANKEE: Easy peasy. Watch this. (*To the AUDIENCE.*) This is a little trick you could try at home, boys and girls. I take one egg . . .

WISHEE: One egg . . .

TWANKEE: I take one plate . . .

WISHEE: One plate . . .

TWANKEE: I throw the egg into the air . . .

(*She does. Drumroll.*)

TWANKEE: . . . and catch it on the . . .

(*The egg splatters on the plate. WISHEE falls about.*)

WISHEE:	This time, I'll help you. I'll throw the egg – you catch it.
TWANKEE:	You throw the egg and I catch it?
WISHEE:	Right. Here we go . . . One . . . Two . . . Three . . .

(*Drumroll. WISHEE throws a pot egg. TWANKEE holds out the plate which shatters into fragments.*)

TWANKEE:	(*Throwing bits of egg and broken plate into the bowl*) Oh, let's get on with it. Now beat it.

(*WISHEE is deeply hurt and turns to leave.*)

TWANKEE:	Where are you going?
WISHEE:	(*Tearfully*) You said beat it.
TWANKEE:	You know what I meant. Beat the eggs.
WISHEE:	Oh . . . (*He produces a huge hammer and swings it back over his head.*)
TWANKEE:	(*Struggling with him*) No no, stupid. Not with a hammer.
WISHEE:	(*Struggling*) Please?
TWANKEE:	No.
WISHEE:	(*Still struggling*) Pretty please?
TWANKEE:	No.

(*WISHEE calms down at last.*)

TWANKEE:	Now drop it.

(*WISHEE drops it (apparently) on TWANKEE'S foot.*)

TWANKEE:	(*Hopping around*) Ah! Now Wishee. Will you please use your head?

(*WISHEE plunges his head into the bowl and pounds the mixture. He comes out covered with flour.*)

TWANKEE:	Right. Now season it.

ACT ONE

(WISHEE sneezes hugely into the bowl. She hits him.)

TWANKEE: Honestly! How can we possibly give that to anyone now? *(Considers.)* They'll never know. Now, are the sausages ready?

(WISHEE brings out a tray of sausages and places them on the table.)

TWANKEE: I don't like the look of these sausages. Look a bit lively to me. *(To the AUDIENCE.)* I want you to keep an eye on those sausages while I read my recipe. If you see any of them move, I want you to shout "You naughty naughty sausage". What d'you mean, you feel silly? How d'you think I feel? Now then . . . *(She takes the recipe book, reading, with her back to the sausages.)* Marinate the raspberries in a . . .

(The trick sausage stands up (with "Swannee" whistle accompaniment). The AUDIENCE shout. TWANKEE spins round to look at the sausage but it lies down and she misses it. She returns to reading.)

TWANKEE: Leave them in brandy for seven years to fully absorb the . . .

(The sausage stands up. The AUDIENCE shouts. TWANKEE spins round. The sausage lies down. She misses it.)

TWANKEE: . . . the flavour of the . . . *(The sausage stands up again. The AUDIENCE shouts. TWANKEE produces a magnum revolver.)* Make my day, punk . . . *(She shoots the sausage – rimshot in pit – which falls down dead.)* And that's why they call them . . . bangers.

WISHEE: But what about the birthday cake?

TWANKEE: The birthday cake? *(She produces a beautiful, amazingly ornate birthday cake with candles.)* Here's one I prepared earlier. *(She blows and the candles light up – she is suddenly tearful.)* All we need now is for the birthday boy to come home.

WISHEE: Perhaps if we all sang "Happy Birthday . . ."

TWANKEE: Good idea. *(Leading the AUDIENCE.)* All together now . . .

(*All sing "Happy Birthday" and on the word "Aladdin", there is an explosion (**PyroQ. 7**) in the oven – followed by a knocking.*)

TWANKEE: (*Whispers*) There's somebody in the cooker.

WISHEE: (*Whispers*) A gingerbread man?

TWANKEE: Open it.

WISHEE: You open it.

TWANKEE: I'm holding the cake.

WISHEE: (*Taking it from her*) I'll hold the cake.

TWANKEE: Oh . . . Honestly . . .

(*She tiptoes, squeakily, to the oven. It flies open and ALADDIN steps out.*)

TWANKEE: Aladdin, my darling boy, how did you get in there?

ALADDIN: I'm not quite sure. But look what I've brought you, Mother.

(*He empties bags of jewels onto the table.*)

TWANKEE: Oh look – wine gums . . .

ALADDIN: Jewels, Mother. We're rich. We'll never go hungry again.

TWANKEE: Rich? (*Putting on ear rings, necklace, crown.*) I could go to the Bridgwater Carnival.

WISHEE: With all that, you could *be* the Bridgwater Carnival.

ALADDIN: I'm going to pay off all our debts, Mother, buy homes and food for all the children, and then I mean to go to the Emperor and ask for the Princess's hand in marriage.

TWANKEE: Eaugh! (*Holding the magic lamp at arm's length.*) But what's this awful old thing? Whyever did you bring it? I'm not having such a filthy object in my house. I shall chuck it away on the rubbish heap at once.

ALADDIN: No, Mother . . .

TWANKEE: What else could I do with it? Out it goes this minute! (*She swings it as if to throw it off stage.*)

AUDIENCE: NO!

TWANKEE: No? What you mean no? Who'm you telling no to? What shall I do with it then? Rub it? Rub what? Oh the lamp? I'm not touching it more than to chuck it away. Here, Aladdin, you brought it in here. If anybody's going to give it a polish, it ought to be you.

ALADDIN: Alright. It might come up quite nice and shiny with a bit of a rub.

(*He rubs the lamp with his sleeve. A crash of thunder, (SQ.16; PyroQ.6; LXQ.44) flashes of lightning. A huge flash and the JINI appears, a towering figure on the welsh dresser.*)

TWANKEE: It's Pavarotti (*or whoever*)...!

ALADDIN: Who are you?

JINI: I am the Jini of the Lamp and at your service, Master. Your every command shall be obeyed and whatever you require shall be brought to you from the far corners of the universe.

TWANKEE: (*Weakly*) Ooh, my nerves. All I want's a cup of tea.

(*The JINI claps his hands. A cup of tea appears in TWANKEE'S hand.*)

TWANKEE: Oh look – Quickbrew. Can you do that with anything?

JINI: I can bring anything that my master commands me to bring. I will comb the Universe to fetch him his heart's desire.

TWANKEE: But who is your master?

JINI: Now it is Aladdin. I belong to whoever owns the lamp.

TWANKEE: You're a sitting tenant then?

JINI: Tell me, mighty Aladdin. What is your heart's desire?

ALADDIN: All I wish at this moment is that Princess Jasmine was here.

(*The JINI claps his hands. A Flash.* (**LXQ.45; PyroQ.7**) *JASMINE appears, reading a book and looking surprised.*)

JASMINE: Aladdin...

ALADDIN: Jasmine. (*To the JINI.*) So you really *can* do anything?

JINI: Anything my master commands.

ALADDIN: Now our problems really *are* over. Now I can go to the Emperor, your father and *demand* to marry you.

JASMINE: But... (*Pointing nervously at the JINI.*) who *is* that? I don't understand.

ALADDIN: I'll explain later. For now, I'm just too happy. Call up all my friends. Children...

WISHEE: (*Calling*) Hey, kids... Aladdin's home... He's safe! And rich!

(*The PEKINESE rush on, cheering, and embrace ALADDIN.*)

ALADDIN: Yes. See, everybody, we're rich. You need never go hungry or homeless again...

(**LXQ.46; FSQ.12**)

Song: ACT ONE FINALE – (*Gounod's "Faust"*)

ALADDIN & JASMINE:
TOGETHER!
FOREVER!
WITH THE ONE I ADORE!
HAND IN HAND, WE WILL FIND –
HAPPINESS EVERMORE!

(*A Flash DL.* (**PyroQ.8**) *ABANAZAR appears.*)

ABANAZAR: NOT SO FAST!

(*A Flash DR.* (**PyroQ.9**) *THYLVIA appears.*)

THYLVIA: I'M AGHAST!

ABANAZAR: THEY WILL NEVER BE UNITED!

THYLVIA: ON YOUR BIKE! YOU'RE NOT INVITED!

ABANAZAR: I RANT! I RAGE!

THYLVIA: YOU'RE TOO LATE – THEY'RE ENGAGED!

ALADDIN & JASMINE: O, WHAT RAPTURE AND BLISS
IS OURS WITH ONE KISS!
ALL OUR FRIENDS ATTENDING IN THEIR FINEST ARRAY
ALL FOR OUR WEDDING DAY!

ABANAZAR: NO! PALTRY FOOLS!
YOUR FOE – ABANAZAR RULES!

THYLVIA: AWAY! BATHE BEATHT, WE CALL –
I THAY – LOVE CONQUERTH ALL!

(LXQ.47)

ALADDIN & JASMINE: LOVE ETERNAL RULES OVER ALL;
WHO CARES WHAT DANGERS MAY BEFALL?
WHATEVER FICKLE FATE SETS BEFORE US,
ONE KISS WILL CAST THE SPELL TO RESTORE US.
LET THE TEMPEST THUNDER AND ROAR,
OUR LOVE WILL LIVE FOR EVER MORE!

THYLVIA: WHERE ITH THY THTING?
LOVE ITH KING!

ALADDIN & JASMINE (*and all except THYLVIA and ABANAZAR*):

LOVE ETERNAL RULES OVER ALL;
WHO CARES WHAT DANGERS MAY BEFALL?

THYLVIA: WUB YOUR WING!
LOVE ITH KING!

ENSEMBLE: WHATEVER –

ABANAZAR: SEE IF I CARE

ENSEMBLE: FICKLE FATE SETS BEFORE US/THEM,

THYLVIA: LOVE ITH KING!
BEGONE! YOU'RE OUT OF YOUR HEAD!

ABANAZAR: ALL SHALL BE MINE!
YOU WASTE YOUR TIME!

ENSEMBLE: WHATEVER FICKLE FATE SETS BEFORE US –
ONE KISS WILL CAST THE SPELL TO RESTORE US.

ABANAZAR: THEY WILL NOT EVER BE WED!

(LXQ.48; FSQ.12A)

ENSEMBLE: LOVE ETERNAL RULES OVER ALL,

THYLVIA: TIME TO HIKE!
ON YOUR BIKE!

ABANAZAR: WHY DON'T YOU SLING YOUR HOOK?
THEY'RE IN SHTOOK!

THYLVIA: THEE WHAT A LOVELY BWIDE THE'LL BE!

ENSEMBLE: WHO CARES WHAT DANGERS MAY BEFALL?

ABANAZAR: ABANAZAR RULES!

ENSEMBLE: WHATEVER FICKLE FATE SETS BEFORE US/THEM,

THYLVIA: HOOWAY! HOOWAY!
FOR THEIR WEDDING DAY!

ENSEMBLE: ONE KISS WILL CAST THE SPELL TO RESTORE US/
THEM.

ABANAZAR: BUT LET'S TAKE
A LITTLE BREAK.
TIME FOR CRISPS AND CHOCS AND ICE-CREAM IN THE
FOYER!

ENSEMBLE: LET THE TEMPEST THUNDER AND ROAR,

ABANAZAR: AND I THINK
I NEED A DRINK!
THERE'S AN INTERVAL FIRST

ENSEMBLE: OUR/THEIR LOVE WILL LIVE FOR EVER MORE!

ABANAZAR: THEN I'LL RETURN TO DO – MY WORST!

(LQ.49; FSQ.12B)

(*Blackout. End of Act One.*)

ACT TWO

Scene One

In front of Panto Gauze. Pekin Municipal Park. **(LXQ.50)** *A very pretty and joyful "Chinese scene". Amid clouds of dry ice, the PEKINESE dance while flying kites. The EMPEROR, ALADDIN (now very richly dressed) and JASMINE, move among them.*

THYLVIA appears before the gauze to tinkly music.

(LXQ.51; FSQ.13)

THYLVIA: All theems thet fair
For the happy pair
And evwything ith heading
Towardth the day –
Not far away –
Of a wegular woyal wedding.
Evewyone'th contented,
The Empewor'th conthented
To Aladdin ath hith thon.
They've made their planth
And called the banth
And Thylvia'th work ith done.

*(A crack of Thunder **(SQ.16)** and a Flash. **(PyroQ.13; LXQ.52; FSQ.14)** ABANAZAR appears DL.)*

ABANAZAR: Best be wary,
You Eastern fairy,
I've not thrown in the towel.
I've had a mull
In the intervul
And come up with something foul.
I'm most impressed
By that pert Princess
And shall have her as my wife
So now I'll wrench
Both the lamp and wench
And take Aladdin's life.

THYLVIA: How thly! How bathe!

ABANAZAR: Oh theut your fathe.
It'th Abanathar'th turn.

Oh curth! Oh dwat it!
You've got me at it.

THYLVIA: I thee I mutht be thtern!
Avaunt! Away!

ABANAZAR: You've had your day.
I've a cunning plan devised.
I'm off to see toe –
My incognito.
You won't know me when I'm ... disguised. (*He goes off DL, guffawing.*)

(*LXQ.53; FSQ.14A*)

THYLVIA: Well, I mutht thay. I'm thurpwithed! (*Exits DR.*)

(*The Gauze flies out* (***FlyQ.7; LXQ.54; FSQ.13A***) *for kite and lion dance.*)

EMPEROR: (*to ALADDIN*) Well, my boy, you've set my mind at rest.

(*Music. TWANKEE enters UC in an extravagant outfit with a diamond-encrusted head dress and a parasol.*)

TWANKEE: (*Tearfully*) Aladdin! Aladdin! My little boy. Marrying and leaving his Mum! It seems like only yesterday that you were under my feet and now you'll soon be off my hands ... Oh dear ... I always cry at weddings – I absolutely howled at mine.

ALADDIN: Alright, Mother, don't carry on so. Your Imperial Majesty, this is my mother ...

TWANKEE: Charmed, I'm sure, your Mint Imperial ... Do you like my jewels?

EMPEROR: Your jewels?

TWANKEE: Yes. Mind, these are just my Summer diamonds. Some are diamonds and some are not.

EMPEROR: Extraordinary! (*To ALADDIN.*) Yet I see that, though you're the son of a common laundress ...

TWANKEE: Steady ...

EMPEROR: A low-class washerwoman ...

TWANKEE: D'you mind?

EMPEROR: A regular old scrubber...

TWANKEE: I'll have you know that I come from a very old Bedminster family. The Pratts. The Pratts are very big in Bedminster and I was a Pratt before I was married.

EMPEROR: Well, whatever your antecedents, madam, your son is certainly a fit husband for my dearest daughter. I rely on you, Aladdin, to take great care of her. She's the apple of my eye and if anything happened to her, my fury would be terrible to behold.

TWANKEE: (*Giving him her parasol and bending down – car horn in pit*) Well, be holding this for me while I tie my shoe.

ALADDIN: I shall keep her safe, sire.

EMPEROR: But tell me – where will you live?

JASMINE: I shan't mind where we live.

EMPEROR: Time enough to decide that after your nuptials. Well, duty calls. Come daughter...

JASMINE: Goodbye, Aladdin...

ALADDIN: Goodbye, Jasmine...

EMPEROR: (*He approaches the flower*) Now that's a plant I've never seen before. I think I shall have that dug up and stuffed for the Imperial Museum.

AUDIENCE: Save the failiah!

EMPEROR: (*Starting back*) Extraordinary...! (*He and JASMINE exit DR.*)

TWANKEE: His Emperorship has a point though. Where will you live? You can't bring a princess to live in a laundry. You'll need a palace.

ALADDIN: We thought a cottage in the country – close to the Great Wall.

TWANKEE:	Cottage be blowed. We're talking lavish here. Get that Jini onto it.
ALADDIN:	Alright. I suppose I should . . .
	(*He rubs the lamp. There is a Flash.* (**PyroQ.14; LXQ.55**) *The JINI appears looking depressed.*)
JINI:	(*Gloomily*) What is your command, Master.
TWANKEE:	What's the matter with you?
JINI:	Been rubbed up the wrong way.
ALADDIN:	The Princess and I will need somewhere to live.
TWANKEE:	And we're not talking Wimpy. Make it big.
ALADDIN:	Mother. We don't want anything too elaborate.
TWANKEE:	Oh yes we do. If you've got it, flaunt it. Now what have you got in the palace line?
JINI:	We do palaces in three sizes.
TWANKEE:	We'll have the biggest then. And we'll need a granny flat for me. So, let's have a shufti.
JINI:	Where do you wish this palace to appear?
TWANKEE:	Over there at the far end of the park – away from the Pekin ducks.
	(*The JINI claps his hands majestically. There is a Flash.* (**PyroQ.15**) *Rumbling music and smoke. An ornate palace grows up out of the ground behind the balustrade.*)
TWANKEE:	Call that big?
	(*The JINI claps. Another wing is added.*)
TWANKEE:	No no. More than that.
ALADDIN:	But Mother . . .
TWANKEE:	You keep quiet – Mother knows best.
	(*JINI claps. Another wing.*)

WISHEE:	I think it needs a tower – or two . . .

(The JINI claps and two minarets grow up.)

TWANKEE:	Or three . . . or four . . . or maybe more . . .

(He claps. Two more minarets.)

WISHEE:	And peacocks. They always have peacocks at palaces . . .

(Two peacocks appear on the roof and spread their tails.)

WISHEE:	And a fountain?

(A fountain begins to play. The JINI is getting tired.)

ALADDIN:	That's enough now . . .
TWANKEE:	No it isn't. I need something to remind me of my home in Brissle.

(Clifton Suspension Bridge slides up between two of the towers and lights up.)

TWANKEE:	Lovely. I love suspenders.
ALADDIN:	I give up. I'm off to meet the Princess . . . *(He exits L.)*
TWANKEE:	Here. It won't be cold, will it?

*(The JINI, exhausted, claps and smoke (**PyroQ.16**) rises from the chimney.)*

TWANKEE:	That looks very nice. Modest but nice. Thank you, Mr Jini . . .

(The JINI crawls off on all fours.)

TWANKEE:	Come, Wishee. Let's go and have a look inside. If anybody wants me, I shall be in my boudoir.

(TWANKEE and WISHEE exit URC as ALADDIN and JASMINE enter DL followed by ABANAZAR wearing a postman's hat.)

(LXQ.56)

JASMINE:	But why must you go?

ALADDIN:	I just got a message. (*Giving ABANAZAR a coin.*) Thank you, postman.
ABANAZAR:	Thank *you*, young sir . . . (*He exits cackling.*)
ALADDIN:	It says that my old grandmother is being turned out of her home. I promised I'd care for her and protect her and now's my chance to keep that promise.
JASMINE:	Oh dear. Will you be gone very long?
ALADDIN:	No time at all. I'll be back before sunset.
ABANAZAR:	(*Appearing round the prosc, DL*) Little does he know what plot I've planned And what nasty weather I have near at hand.
THYLVIA:	(*Appearing round prosc, DR*) Yet he thall thurvive the thavagetht thtorm With twue love – and Thylvia – to keep him warm.

(*FSQ.15*)

        Song: Duet (*ALADDIN and JASMINE*)

(*FSQ.15A*)

Evening. Strings of Chinese lanterns glow. ABANAZAR enters L, wearing a cloak and a huge hat as a disguise. He carries a basket filled with shiny new lamps – similar to the magic lamp.

ABANAZAR:	New lamps for old. New lamps for old. Special offer. New lamps for old. (*To AUDIENCE.*) Hush. You're so predictable. Hissed again. But how in Hades did you recognise me? Nobody can see through this cunning disguise . . .
PEKE:	(*Passing*) Evening, Abanazar . . .
ABANAZAR:	Peasant.
PEKE:	Wrinkly.

        (*Other PEKES enter with old lamps and torches of all sorts. ABANAZAR begins to exchange them. PONG enters with a battered blue police lamp.*)

ABANAZAR: Bring out your old lamps. This offer is free
And every new lamp has my own guarantee.
New lamps for old!

JASMINE: (*Entering UC – to PONG*) What's going on?

PING: It's an old pedlar offering new lamps for old. You bring him any old lamp and he gives you a new one.

JASMINE: Aladdin's got a lamp. I don't know where he got it but it's a battered old thing that doesn't seem to work.

PONG: Right. Now's your chance to surprise him and get him a shiny new one.

JASMINE: I'm not sure I should. It's not mine after all.

PONG: You don't get a chance like this everyday, your Highness.

JASMINE: Well . . I'll go and see if I can find it.

PONG: (*Now at the front of the queue – to ABANAZAR*) Have you got one that makes a wailing sound?

ABANAZAR: Wailing sound . . . yes . . . here . . . (*He gives PONG a large rubber torch then goes on exchanging lamps.*)

(*PONG moves off, switches on the torch and listens – nothing – shakes it a few times – returns to ABANAZAR.*)

PONG: Excuse me . . .

ABANAZAR: What is it now?

PONG: This doesn't make a wailing sound.

(*ABANAZAR takes the torch, examines it, and hits PONG on the head. PONG wails like a police syren.*)

ABANAZAR: Works perfectly.

(*Music. TWANKEE enters as a parody of Suzy Wong, carrying a standard lamp.*)

ABANAZAR: But wait. Who comes here? 'Tis that stupid woman, I can't abide.
Yet, if I can woo the trollop to my side,
She can steal the lamp and bring me joy untold.

New lamps for old. New lamps for old.

TWANKEE: Oh hello, Abergavenny.

ABANAZAR: (*Furious*) Abanazar!

TWANKEE: Coo, you should get that washed dear, don't half niff.

ABANAZAR: New lamps for old. New lamps for old.

TWANKEE: Alright, dear. Don't go on. What sort of lamps? Oil lamps, headlamps, gig-lamps? Or does this come up to your standard? (*Indicates standard lamp.*)

ABANAZAR: It's a very special lamp I seek. Oh, Widow Twankee please help me. (*Coming on strong.*) Help me and I'll make you the happiest woman in Pekin. You'll win our special offer – a world cruise.

TWANKEE: Ooo. My favourite – Club 18/30.

ABANAZAR: Twenty years too late. Be mine. Be mine. You must be mine!

TWANKEE: Oh Aberdovey, you set a woman's heart aflutter. You're so masterful – like a marauding Viking. I sometimes wish I'd lived in the Dark Ages.

ABANAZAR: (*Aside*) You certainly look terrible in the light. (*To her.*) Don't move. That profile. Such a pretty chin.

TWANKEE: I know. I liked it so much I ordered two more.

ABANAZAR: Has your face been lifted?

TWANKEE: They couldn't seem to manage that so they lowered my body.

ABANAZAR: You're... beautiful, Widow Twankee.

TWANKEE: I do love a man who's frank.

ABANAZAR: Lucky for me I'm Abanazar. But what's a nice girl like you doing in a place like this?

TWANKEE: Oh just meandering. Taking in the air.

ABANAZAR: Oh my little lotus blossom. I just knew it was you when I heard the dry tread of your Doc Martins. (*Embracing her.*) Oh my little piccolo. I could play such tunes on you if you'd let me. (*Aside.*) It's like chatting up a chip butty. (*To her.*) Age shall not wither them.

TWANKEE: Age is a question of mind over matter. If you don't mind, it doesn't matter.

ABANAZAR: Oh, Widow Twankee, please. I want you for my wife.

TWANKEE: Don't be silly. What'd your wife want with me.

ABANAZAR: I mean I want you to *be* my wife.

TWANKEE: Do you mean it? I'm flabbergasted.

(*He grabs her round the waist.*)

TWANKEE: Oh my flabbers've been ghasted.

ABANAZAR: Oh my lovely one. Share your knick knacks with me please.

TWANKEE: I wouldn't share my knick knacks with anybody – let alone you.

ABANAZAR: Please.

TWANKEE: Oh . . . Well . . . If I gave you my photo, would you wear it in a locket round your neck?

ABANAZAR: Forever.

TWANKEE: (*Giving him a photo*) Here you are then. Mind, that photo doesn't do me justice.

ABANAZAR: (*Looking at the photo*) It's mercy you need, not justice. (*Throws it away.*)

TWANKEE: Do you really want to be friends?

ABANAZAR: Yes.

TWANKEE: Really.

ABANAZAR: Yes.

TWANKEE: Really really really.

ABANAZAR: Yes yes yes.

TWANKEE: Bosom buddies? (*She clasps him to her.*)

ABANAZAR: Yes.

TWANKEE: I hope you're not trying to trifle with my affections or make a custard of my heart.

ABANAZAR: Never. D'you know . . . (*He turns on the standard lamp, (**LXQ.57; FSQ.16**) kneels beneath it, and sings.*)

    IF YOU WERE THE ONLY GIRL IN THE WORLD.

TWANKEE: AND YOU WERE THE ONLY BOY –

ABANAZAR: NOTHING ELSE WOULD MATTER IN THIS WORLD
                                                             TODAY –

TWANKEE: WE COULD GO ON LOVING IN THE SAME OLD WAY.

ABANAZAR: A GARDEN OF EDEN, JUST MADE FOR TWO

TWANKEE: WITH NOTHING TO MAR OUR JOY.

ABANAZAR: I WOULD SAY SUCH WONDERFUL THINGS TO YOU –

TWANKEE: THERE WOULD BE SUCH WONDERFUL THINGS TO DO . . .

ABANAZAR: IF YOU WERE THE ONLY GIRL IN THE WORLD –

TWANKEE: AND YOU WERE THE ONLY BOY . . .

(*LXQ.58; FSQ.16A*)

ABANAZAR: Oh, Widow Twankee – dearest – fetch me the lamp!

TWANKEE: (*Pushing him over*) So that's it! Lamps. That's all you men care about. That's all you want from us girls – our lamps! (*To the AUDIENCE.*) Isn't that right, girls? It's just lamps all the time with them, isn't it? Lamps lamps lamps. They turn us on and fiddle with our reflectors. They burn up our oil and prick our wicks. And then what do they do? Cast us aside – snuffed!

ABANAZAR: But, my dear Widow Twankee!

TWANKEE: Oh... (*Snatching up her standard lamp.*) Go trim your wick and buff up your reflector! (*She goes.*)

ABANAZAR: Curses. Stupid woman. Can't she see what a nice, warm, loveable, upright, honest, deeply wonderful person I am? (*To the AUDIENCE.*) You think I'm lovable, don't you?

AUDIENCE: NO.

ABANAZAR: Well bubbles to the lot of you then. And now I've given away all my new lamps but this one and...

(*JASMINE is heard singing off UC.*)

ABANAZAR: But stay... Here comes that pretty princess... New lamps for old. New lamps for old. Easy terms...

JASMINE: Excuse me...

ABANAZAR: Yes my dear? (*Aside.*) Egad, so young and lovely. A fitting bride indeed for the Master of the Universe. She must be mine. (*To her.*) You seem worried, my child...

JASMINE: I don't know whether I should exchange this lamp. I think that my fiancee is very fond of it.

ABANAZAR: Ah but think how much fonder he'll be of this fine new lamp I have here. See how it glitters and gleams.

JASMINE: Do you think I should?

ABANAZAR: Of course you should.

JASMINE: Should I?

AUDIENCE: NO!

JASMINE: No. No. I don't think I should...

ABANAZAR: Take a chance. Kick over the traces.
(*To the AUDIENCE.*) And, as for you lot, shut your faces. See. Look here, my child. (*Making passes over the lamp.*)
Lamp so lovely. Lamp so bright –
Show to us your glittering light.

(*The lamp lights up.*)

JASMINE: (*Delighted*) Oh. It's lovely, isn't it?

ABANAZAR:	And think how delighted Ala . . . your fiancee – whatever his name is – will be. And I'll throw in our special-offer antique-style nut crackers.
JASMINE:	(*Uncertain*) Well . . .
ABANAZAR:	. . . and genuine Badgerline buspass . . .
JASMINE:	(*Dithering*) Well . . .
ABANAZAR:	. . . and a year's subscription to "Hello" magazine.
JASMINE:	(*Decided*) I'll take it.
ABANAZAR:	You'll never regret it. Never . . . Because . . . When I am King of the Universe, you'll be the Queen at my side . . .
JASMINE:	What? But . . . Who *are* you?
ABANAZAR:	I knew I'd fool you with my disguise. Now what can I say but "surprise, surprise!"

(*He throws off his hat.*)

JASMINE:	(*Recognising him*) Abanazar! You! (*She tries to run.*)
ABANAZAR:	(*Seizing her wrist*) Stay, my proud beauty. I want to make you an offer you can't refuse . . .
JASMINE:	(*Struggling helplessly*) Let go of me, vile brute . . . Let me go!
ABANAZAR:	Congratulations, Princess, a job well done. We'll share a future of endless fun.
JASMINE:	Ah, what a fool I've been. What a blind fool! What will Aladdin say? (*Breaking free.*) Let me *go!* (*Rushing off to the palace.*) Aladdin! Aladdin!
ABANAZAR:	Yes. Go to your palace and stay within. One rub of me lamp and the plan'll begin. (*Rubbing the lamp.*) Oh Jini appear – sim salavin!

(*A Flash.* (**PyroQ.17; LXQ.59**) *The JINI appears up through the stage* (*if possible*), *cheerfully majestic.*)

JINI:	Oh . . . what is your command, Aladdin of the Lamp?

Oh . . . mighty Aladdin!
(Sees ABANAZAR.) Oh . . . blimey!

ABANAZAR: Yes. Tis I. *I* am your master now and I'll soon show you what hard work really is.

JINI: That's one thing I hate about this job – nothing but takeover bids!

ABANAZAR: You must obey me whether you like it or not.

JINI: I'll obey you – but I won't like it.

ABANAZAR: Then lump it! First, I want you to take the palace with the Princess and all that's in it to the Sahara Desert.

JINI: The Sahara? That wild and desolate waterless place from which no wanderer returns? What would you want with that young and beautiful, tender, desirable slip of a Princess in such a place?

ABANAZAR: *(Cackles)* Just do as I say.

JINI: *(Depressed)* I must obey.

ABANAZAR: Too right you must. So now – away!

JINI: *(Trying to generate enthusiasm)* I go. I go. Look how I go. Swift as an arrow from a Tartar's bow.

(He plods off. Lightning, wind and thunder **(SQ.17; LXQ.60)** *during:)*

ABANAZAR: Come, tempests, blow!
Lash, hail and snow!
Lightning and thunder, conflate!
Let the hurricane
Proclaim my name –
Abanazar – known as the Great!

(The palace shakes and begins to rise. **(FlyQ.10; LXQ.61)** *During the following, it flies out, apparently borne up by a tiny puppet version of the JINI.)*

ABANAZAR: Transport the Hall –
Princess and all –
To the desolate Sahara.
Where I'll cover her

With silk and fur
And a million pound tiara.
(*Megalomania sets in rapidly.*) From pole to pole,
I'm in control
And right round the Equator.
I'll be a beast
From west to east –
Far worse than Terminator.
(*To the AUDIENCE.*) And, as for you –
You hideous crew –
I'll teach you to obey.
When I'm next in town,
You must all bow down,
Cos Abanazar Rules! OK?

(*He sweeps off UC, guffawing maniacally. ALADDIN enters DL, fighting against the storm.*)

ALADDIN: What a dreadful storm. I could hardly find my way. The path from the mountains was washed away and an avalanche blocked the pass. I can't wait to get back to the Princess and the warmth and welcome of the Palace . . . I . . . (*Seeing the empty space.*) What's this? The palace! It isn't there anymore. It's . . . gone!!

(*A fanfare.*) (**LXQ.62**) (*The EMPEROR enters in a rage followed by PONG and the PEKINESE. The storm dies away.*)

EMPEROR: Yes, Aladdin, wicked whelp! The palace has vanished and, with it, my dearest and most cherished child who I gave into your safe keeping. This is your villainy. Seize him!

(*PONG seizes ALADDIN and fixes on manacles.*)

ALADDIN: But, sire . . .

EMPEROR: No pleading. No lame excuses. You – Pong. Take down his particulars.

PONG: Right. You heard – get 'em off.

EMPEROR: No no, you fool. Where's that Ping? He's never here when you want him. Now, boy, an explanation is in order.

ALADDIN: I have none, sire. That wicked Abanazar lies behind this, I'm sure. He must have kidnapped the Princess . . .

EMPEROR: It's useless to blame this Abanazar. I entrusted her to your care and you left her unguarded.

ALADDIN: I will search every corner of the world, sire. I love your daughter and I will never rest until she is safely returned.

EMPEROR: You will not be at liberty to search. Your love is worthless. Throw him into prison.

ALADDIN: But sire . . .

EMPEROR: Into prison. (*To AUDIENCE.*) He deserves it, does he not?

AUDIENCE: NO!

EMPEROR: Well I say he does and, in Pekin, what I say – goes. Take him away!

(*Blacks drawn on. A single spot on the EMPEROR DR (**LXQ.63**) while ALADDIN is fastened into chains lit by a Cell-bars gobo DC.*)

EMPEROR: Hear me, all peoples of China and all you barbarians of the outside world! Let it be known by my edict that, this twenty-eighth day of Marbarry in this year of the monkey, 1233, that whosoever finds the Princess Jasmine and restores her safely to me shall be given her hand in marriage.

(*Barred light (**LXQ.64**) comes up on ALADDIN for:*)

Scene Two

The Imperial Prison.

ALADDIN: It wasn't my fault the palace disappeared. I bet it was that wicked Abanazar up to his tricks again. I must get free and set off to rescue the Princess. But how can I get out of these chains and this dungeon?

(*A sign appears round the prosc. DR saying "WUB YOUR WING".*)

AUDIENCE: WUB YOUR WING!

ALADDIN: Of course. The ring! Maybe the Slave of the Ring could help me. It's worth a shot.

(*He rubs the ring. THYLVIA wanders on DR with a half-eaten ice-lolly.*)

THYLVIA: Aladdin, weally! What can I thay?
I can't leave you alone for a thingle day.
(*Licking fingers.*) I put my feet up for a quiet minute
And, when I look, you're right back in it.

ALADDIN: I'm sorry, Sylvia, but the Princess has vanished. It can mean only one thing. Abanazar has kidnapped her.

THYLVIA: Abanathar? That gwuethome thavage?
We mutht move fatht before the'th wavithed.

ALADDIN: Yes we must. Please help me, Sylvia.

THYLVIA: Eathy peathy. Jutht thay the magic wordth.

ALADDIN: But what *are* the magic wordth . . . words?

THYLVIA: Thimple. But we'll need all our fwiendth to help – to bootht the power you know.

ALADDIN: I'm sure they will. Just tell us what to say.

THYLVIA: Ithy withy alacatham.
Thauthage wollth and thtwawbewwy jam!

ALADDIN: You're having us on.

THYLVIA: Thertainly not. (*Handing him her ice-lolly.*) Hold my Thoom. Come on now . . . (*Leading the audience.*) Come on. Thpeak up. To thave Aladdin and the Pwintheth!

THYLVIA & AUDIENCE: Ithy withy alacatham.
Thauthage wolls and thtwawbewwy jam!

(*There is a Flash (**PyroQ.18**) and ALADDIN'S chains fall to the ground.*)

ALADDIN: Oh, thanks friends. But what do I do now? Where shall I begin to look for the Princess? Where has Abanazar taken her?

AUDIENCE: The Sahara.

ALADDIN: What? Where?

Act Two

AUDIENCE:	The Sahara!
ALADDIN:	The Sahara? Where's that?
KNOW-ALLS IN AUDIENCE:	Africa.
ALADDIN:	Africa? Then it's hopeless. How can I possibly get to Africa in time to save her?
THYLVIA:	The Thahara'th far too far to walk – a twip to make you quaver. You'd even fail on a Bwitith Wail Awayday Thuper-Thaver. But I can help you yet again and, if we make it tharp it Thouldn't take you long at all – on my vewy own . . .

(*The magic carpet flies in down a moonbeam.*) (**FlyQ.11; LXQ.65**)

THYLVIA:	Magic Carpet!!
ALADDIN:	That's wonderful What do I do?
THYLVIA:	Jutht pile aboard. Get it? Pile aboard? Oh, pleathe yourthelveth.

(*ALADDIN sits on the carpet.*)

THYLVIA:	Thith will fly you, thteered by the thtarth. Turn tharp wight at Pluto and left at Marth. Then, below, you'll thee her – the Pwintheth of your pwayer – Thtwaight down thwough the hole in the othone layer. (*Leading the audience.*) Five. Four. Three. Two. One. Ignithion!

(*The carpet rises and hovers.*) (**FlyQ.12**)

THYLVIA:	Blatht off!

(*With soaring music, the carpet rises majestically.*) (**FlyQ.13**)

ALADDIN:	Goodbye, Sylvia, and thank you. And thank you all for helping me to escape.
THYLVIA:	Thank you for flying Thylvia Carpetth. Have a nithe day . . .

(Blackout.) **(LXQ.66)** **(FlyQ.14; SQ.18; LXQ.67)**

Scene Three

The Dungeon of ALADDIN'S Palace – now in the Sahara.

Swirling mist, water dripping, eerie light. A grill in the floor C with red and green light and sinister shadows coming up from it. WIDOW TWANKEE, the PRINCESS and WISHEE WASHEE are chained to the wall. The chains are (apparently) linked so that, when one of them leans forward the other two are pulled back against the wall.

ALL THREE: (*Sing quietly, rattling chains in time*) "Always look on the bright side of life . . ."

(*A big Spider comes down* **(FlyQ.15)** *on a bungy and goes out again.*)

TWANKEE: I've never seen a yo-yo with legs before.

WISHEE: (*Very dramatic*) Oh woe is me. Oh woe is me. I'm lost. All is bad. Oh woe is me. Oh WOE . . . OH . . .

TWANKEE & JASMINE: Oh . . . Shut up.

TWANKEE: So this is Horfield. Very gloomy in here. It looked alright from a distance – rather like my old age pension – it looks alright from a long way off but it isn't much when you get up to it.

(*ABANAZAR enters R. TWANKEE and WISHEE hiss. The spider drops on his head* **(FlyQ.16)** *and knocks him down. He scrambles up and shakes his fist at the audience.*)

ABANAZAR: So, my proud beauty. Are you ready to yield to my desires? Ready yet to be my blushing bride?

TWANKEE: Well, at my age, you've to take what you can.

ABANAZAR: Not you, Mrs Mangle – this lovely. (*Crossing to JASMINE.*) Well, Princess? Are you ready to walk down the aisle with me?

JASMINE: Never. Never.

ABANAZAR: We'll see about that. We have ways of making you walk. I shall have to use one of my spells!

WISHEE: You're right. There's a terrible niff in here.

ABANAZAR: Not smells – *SSSSP*ELLS!!

WISHEE: Could you spray that again please?

ABANAZAR: I'm known for my magical skills and my (*Roaring.*) POWER!!

WISHEE: Ooo look, you can see the little dangler down his throat.

ABANAZAR: (*Aside*) I must get these two fools to persuade her for me. I shall bend them to my will. I shall put them under my magical mental powers of hypnosis. (*To WISHEE.*) Are you susceptible to hypnosis?

WISHEE: Big noses?

ABANAZAR: Hypnosis, halfwit. Look into my eyes. What do you see?

WISHEE: Eyeballs?

ABANAZAR: Repeat everything I say. You are now under my spell . . .

(*They all begin to sway on their chains.*)

ALL THREE: You are now starting to smell.

ABANAZAR: No no. You are in my power.

ALL: No no. You are in my power.

ABANAZAR: Not in your power, *my* power . . . *stuu* . . . pid!

ALL: Not in your power, *my* power . . . *stuu* . . . pid!

ABANAZAR: Sleeeeep. Sleeeep.

(*They are now swaying more and more.*)

ALL: Sleeeeep. Sleeeeep.

ABANAZAR: You are going to sleep.

ALL: We are going to sleep.

ABANAZAR: You are going ... going ...

ALL: Going ... going ...

TWANKEE: I think I'm coming back again.

ABANAZAR: Shut up. Abracadabra. (*They freeze.*) You know your orders?

TWANKEE: I'll have a spotted dick please.

WISHEE: I'll have a gin and dettol please.

ABANAZAR: It's useless. How can I control your minds when you haven't got any? (*Moving to TWANKEE.*) You're close to an idiot.

TWANKEE: I'll move.

ABANAZAR: Very well, Princess ... If you won't consent to marry me, I shall have to throw you to ... (*he points to the grating in the floor.*) The Thing ... Down ... There ... !

TWANKEE: What thing down where?

(*There is a deafening roar from below.* (**SQ.19; LXQ.68**) *Huge claws and tentacles reach up through the grating accompanied by green smoke.*)

TWANKEE: Oh, *that* thing down *there*.

WISHEE: What's down there then?

ABANAZAR: (*Looking down into the green light, shadows flitting across his face*) I can't tell you. It's too ... horrible ... even for me!

TWANKEE: It *must* be horrible.

ABANAZAR: They call it ...

ALL: Yes ... ?

ABANAZAR: They call it ...

ALL: Yes yes?

ABANAZAR: They call it . . .

ALL: Yes yes yes?

ABANAZAR: The *Thing Down There!*

ALL: Oh.

ABANAZAR: Once it grips you in its gripe you're a gonner. (*Shivers.*) Whooo-oo-ooo!

ALL: (*Shivering*) Whoooo-ooo-ooo!

ABANAZAR: But enough of this . . .

TWANKEE: That's quite enough of this . . .

ABANAZAR: Now, Princess, will you marry me?

JASMINE: Never. Never.

ABANAZAR: Very well. Prepare yourself for . . .

ALL: The Thing Down There?

ABANAZAR: Not yet. That's too horrible – even for me. First – the torture. (*Going off R.*) I'll go and get the paraphenalia.

WISHEE: That'll be for his parafin lamp.

(*ABANAZAR cackles evilly and exits.*)

WISHEE: I didn't think it was that funny. (*To TWANKEE.*) Mind, I thought he fancied you.

TWANKEE: No. It was only puppy love.

WISHEE: How do you know?

TWANKEE: His nose was cold. But what are we going to do?

WISHEE: Nobody knows where we are.

TWANKEE: *We* don't even know where we are.

JASMINE: I'm not afraid. Aladdin will rescue us.

WISHEE: How can he do that if he doesn't know where to look?

(*Music. ALADDIN flies in on the magic carpet.*) (**FlyQ.17**)

TWANKEE: It's the man from Allied Carpets.

JASMINE: It's Aladdin!

(*ALADDIN leaps from the carpet, which flies out again.*) (**FlyQ.18**)

ALADDIN: (*Releasing them*) Don't worry. I'll soon get you out of this.

JASMINE: (*Embracing him*) My hero!

ALADDIN: Where's Abanazar?

TWANKEE: Gone off to get his paraphenalia –

WISHEE: For his parafin lamp.

TWANKEE: Oh shut up.

ALADDIN: Leave it to me. I must find him and get the lamp from him or we'll be for ever in his power. Stay here . . .

TWANKEE: Stay here . . .

ALADDIN: And watch that you aren't grabbed by anything strange and nasty – like monsters, creepy-crawlies, ghosts or ghoulies. I'll be back . . . (*He exits – heroic.*)

WISHEE: What did he say?

TWANKEE: Watch we're not grabbed by ghosts or ghoulies.

WISHEE: I don't mind being grabbed by a ghost but not by the . . .

TWANKEE: That'll do. And we've to keep our eyes peeled for Abanazar.

ALADDIN: (*Returning with the lamp*) Come on, everybody. I got the lamp and he didn't even see me.

ABANAZAR: (*Peering round prosc, DR*) That's what he thinks . . . !

ALADDIN: We must call up the carpet . . .

ACT TWO

ABANAZAR: (*Stepping forward*) Hold!

TWANKEE: Hold what?

ABANAZAR: Not so fast!

ALL: Abanazar!

ABANAZAR: Yes. 'Tis I. The rightful Ruler of the Universe. Now. Give me the lamp. 'Tis mine, 'tis mine.

ALADDIN: We'll see what the Jini has to say about that . . .

(*He is about to rub the lamp but he has backed too close to the grill. A claw reaches up and grabs his ankle* (**SQ.20**) *and, as he falls, the lamp sails through the air and ABANAZAR catches it and is about to rub it when WISHEE tickles him. He screams with laughter and throws the lamp into the air. JASMINE catches it. TWANKEE blows a whistle.*)

MUSIC: MATCH OF THE DAY

(*They form a three quarter line and pass the lamp with ABANAZAR in pursuit. They do some fancy passing until ABANAZAR finally catches it by a foul.*)

ABANAZAR: (*Triumphant*) At last!

(*Again he is about to rub the lamp when the claws reach up and grab him.* (**SQ.21**) *He screams and throws the lamp. ALADDIN catches it. ABANAZAR is fighting for his life.*)

ABANAZAR: Foiled again . . . Ahh! No . . . Not . . . the Thing Down There! No . . . No . . . Aaaaahhhh . . . !

(*The grating opens and he is being dragged down into the depths – re-emerging from time to time, wrestling with different claws and tentacles.*)

ALADDIN: Quick. Whistle for the carpet.

TWANKEE: (*Tries*) RASPBERRY.

WISHEE: *Pathetic whistle.*

JASMINE: (*Fingers in her mouth – a piercing whistle*)

(Music. The carpet flies in.) **(FlyQ.18)**

ALADDIN: Quick, Jasmine. Pile aboard...

WISHEE: *(Falls about)* Pile aboard...!

JASMINE: Come on, Mrs Twankee...

ALADDIN: Come on, Wishee...

TWANKEE: Mind the doors...

WISHEE: Wait for me...

TWANKEE: *(Rolling off)* These privatised carpets... Don't give you time to get on...

(The carpet flies out **(FlyQ.19; SQ.15)** *with ALADDIN and JASMINE aboard and WISHEE and TWANKEE running and jumping after it. ABANAZAR is being finally dragged down to a horrible death as the lights fade to blackout.)* **(LXQ.69)**

(FlyQ.20; LXQ.70)

Scene Four

A Street in Pekin. Mournful music.

The EMPEROR is weeping. PONG is trying to comfort him but is also overcome with grief. The PEKINESE are all sobbing noisily.

EMPEROR: It's no use.

PONG: No.

EMPEROR: She's vanished without trace...

PONG: Yes...

EMPEROR: We'll never see her again...

PONG: No...

EMPEROR: My daughter is lost for ever...

PONG: Yes...

EMPEROR: We shall never... never... see her again...

PONG: Nor Aladdin...

(*The PEKINESE sob louder. THYLVIA skips on DR.*)

THYLVIA: Oh dear, poor dearth,
What floodth of tearth.
(*To a PEKINESE.*) Oh cheer up, little chappie.
For evewy time,
In pantomime,
The ending mutht be happy.
(*To the AUDIENCE.*) But they can't thee
Little magic me.
I'm in another dimenthion.
Tho it'th lucky I've got
The next bit of plot
On thignth for your attenthion.

EMPEROR: Where can they be?

(*THYLVIA brings on an easel with a large sign saying "IN THE MUNITHIPAL PARK".*)

AUDIENCE: In the Munithipal Park.

EMPEROR: Who's in the Park?

(*THYLVIA changes the sign to read 'ALADDIN'.*)

AUDIENCE: Aladdin.

PONG: Aladdin?

(*Sign changes to read: "AND THE PWINTHETH".*)

AUDIENCE: And the Pwintheth.

EMPEROR: My daughter?

(*Sign reads: "YETH".*)

AUDIENCE: Yeth.

PONG: Are you sure?

(*Sign: "THLIP ALONG THWIFTLY AND THEE FOR YOURTHELF".*)

AUDIENCE: Thlip along thwiftly and thee for yourrthelf.

EMPEROR: They're in the Park.

ALL: Hooray . . .

EMPEROR: Alright, everybody. At once. To the Park . . . !

PONG: To the Park . . . !

ALL: To the Park . . . !

(*They all rush off DL as the cloth flies out to reveal:*)

Scene Five

Pekin Municipal Park. They all rush on again from L into the park and stop dead.

PONG: They're not here.

EMPEROR: There's nobody here.

PONG: (*To the AUDINCE*) You were having us on . . .

(*They all advance menacingly on the AUDIENCE.*)

EMPEROR: Right, Pong. Go and get five hundred sets of handcuffs. I'm going to arrest the whole boiling of them for mocking my majesty.

(*PONG runs off R.*)

EMPEROR: I will deal with the grownups. Pekinese, clobber the kids.

(*But he breaks down, sobbing against the prosc. DR as ALADDIN, JASMINE and WISHEE enter from L.*)

ALADDIN: Where's Mother got to?

(*We hear the scream of a diving aircraft (SQ.22) followed by massive crash and tinkle off L. TWANKEE enters in full Biggles outfit with helmet, goggles and wired-up scarf.*)

TWANKEE:	Have you ever tried to park a flying carpet in Broadmead on a Saturday?
JASMINE:	(*Going to him*) Father . . .
EMPEROR:	Don't bother me now, Jasmine. I'm grieving for Jasmine. (*Seeing her.*) Jasmine! It's you!
JASMINE:	Yes, Father. Aladdin came and rescued all of us from that evil Abanazar.
EMPEROR:	My boy, I owe you an apology. How can I ever reward you?
ALADDIN:	By allowing me to marry your daughter, sire.
EMPEROR:	Of course. Of course. Let us prepare for the wedding at once. No more delay. Let tomorrow be your wedding day.
ALL:	HOORAY!
EMPEROR:	But where will you live now that your palace is marooned in the Sahara?
ALADDIN:	I think the Jini will be able to handle that.
	(*He rubs the lamp. A Flash.* (**PyroQ.18; LXQ.72**) *The JINI appears UC.*)
JINI:	Ah. A pleasure to be working for you again, master. What is your desire?
ALADDIN:	I hate to trouble you but could you bring my palace back from the Sahara?
JINI:	Indeed I can. I took the liberty of fitting retro rockets.
	(*He claps his hands. "ZARATHUSTRA" music as the palace descends spectacularly* (**FlyQ.22; PyroQ.19**) *with blazing rockets and settles into its original position.*)
TWANKEE:	I bet he drinks Carling Black Label. But I must slip off and slip into my natty munber for the nuptials. (*Going DL.*)
EMPEROR:	Yes. And now, let everyone prepare for the wedding. Let the bells . . .

ALADDIN

*(There is a crack of thunder **(SQ.23)** and ABANAZAR, a severed claw still clutching at his neck, enters UC brandishing a broadsword.)*

ABANAZAR: *(Hacking off bits of tentacle)* Not so fast, Aladdin.
Again, well met.
But Abanazar isn't beaten yet.
It seems my magic and my evil glare
Were too much – even for the Thing Down There.
(Circling. Menacing.) Though I'm exhausted – nearly out of rhymes –
Come on, Aladdin, for the sake of old times.
(He kicks the Failiah. It squeaks.) **(SQ.24)**
Give me some room, you festering flower
And soon they'll all be back in my power.
I'll fight you with my final breath.
Broadswords, Aladdin, to the death!

(ALADDIN takes the EMPEROR'S sword. Music. A spectacular fight, up and down the stairs, leaping over balustrades, first ABANAZAR is winning (fighting dirty, of course) but, gradually, ALADDIN drives him back. But, when nearly defeated, ABANAZAR seizes JASMINE.)

ABANAZAR: One false move and the girl dies.
Throw down your sword, you Pekin tramp.
Now. Kneel before me with the lamp!

(ALADDIN throws down his sword, takes the lamp from WISHEE and kneels before ABANAZAR. JASMINE rushes to the EMPEROR. The PEKINESE weep as ABANAZAR raises his sword to cut off ALADDIN'S head.)

ABANAZAR: And now . . .

(The Failiah squeaks crossly, **(SQ.25)** *reaches out a tendril and seizes ABANAZAR'S wrist, another tendril coils round his neck. He drops the sword. ALADDIN snatches it up and holds ABANAZAR prisoner.)*

ALL: HOORAY!

EMPEROR: Evil Abanazar, for your wicked deeds and dishonourable intentions, I sentence you to die the death of a thousand cuts while boiling in oil and being eaten slowly by the royal pirhana fish. OR – to marry this winsome widow woman here . . .

(Music. TWANKEE enters, seductive, half veiled, in harem costume, with twirling tassels on her bosom.)

ABANAZAR: *(Overcome, grovelling with gratitude)* Oh, your Majesty... What can I say... I never expected such mercy... Such munificence... such...

(TWANKEE pulls a string and the veil draws aside like a curtain.)

ABANAZAR: AH... No... Widow Twankee.

EMPEROR: I'm sure you'll make the right choice.

ABANAZAR: I shall. Heat up the cauldron... Sharpen the knives... Bring on the pirhana fish. *(He runs off, screaming.)*

EMPEROR: And now – prepare for the wedding. Let the bells ring out!

(They do.)

EMPEROR: Let the trumpets sound!

(They do.)

EMPEROR: Summon all my people for the wedding of my daughter Princess Jasmine to Pekin's very own hero – Aladdin!

(Fireworks explode across the sky **(LXQ.73)** *as they sing:)*

Song: LOVE IS EVERYWHERE (*Reprise*) *(ALL)*
LOVE IS EVERYWHERE –
LIKE A MELODY WITHOUT AN ENDING,
TO ITS STRAINS A MILLION HEARTS ARE BLENDING –
LOVE IS EVERYWHERE.
LOVE IS EVERYWHERE –
IN THE MAGIC MYSTERY OF MOONLIGHT,
IN THE HAUNTING SPLENDOUR OF A JUNE NIGHT,
LOVE IS EVERYWHERE.
NOW BY A STROKE OF CHANCE,
OUR HEARTS HAVE FOUND ROMANCE,
WE'LL DO OUR BEST TO MAKE IT STAY.
AND ALL OUR LIFETIME THROUGH,
OUR LOVE WILL STILL BE TRUE
WHATEVER FATE MAY SEND OUR WAY.
LOVE IS EVERYWHERE –
IN THE WORDS THESE LIPS OF MINE ARE SINGING –
EVEN IN THE DREAMS THE NIGHT IS BRINGING –

LOVE IS EVERYWHERE.
LOVE IS EVERYWHERE!

(Blackout.) **(LXQ. 74)**

(FlyQ. 23; LXQ. 75)

Scene Six

A Street in Pekin.

(FSQ. 17)

Songsheet.

ALADDIN'S GOT THE LAMP!
ALADDIN'S GOT THE LAMP!
EE-I-ADDY-O
ALADDIN'S GOT THE LAMP!

(LXQ. 76; FSQ. 17A)

Scene Seven

Walkdown and Calls. **(FSQ. 17B)**

Finale:

ALL: WHATEVER –
FORTUNE MAY HAVE BEEN SENDING,
WE NEVER
DOUBTED THIS HAPPY ENDING.
WE KNEW IT – DIDN'T YOU?
A REWARD FOR LOVE THAT'S TRUE.
PROCLAIM IT!
AND LET NO-ONE DOUBT IT.
A SHAME IT –
WOULD BE TO BE WITHOUT IT
FOR LOVE IS ALL
AS YOU MAY RECALL
WHEN THE CURTAIN'S DUE.

THYLVIA –
BELIEVE IT, WILL YA –
TOOK A COURSE IN . . .
WELL YOU SURELY CAN GUESS –

THYLVIA: A COURSE IN – ELOCUTION!
YES YES I CAN SAY "S"
MAY I STRESS MY PROWESS?
I HOPE I IMPRESS!

ALL: SO NOW WE
WISH YOU WARM SEASON'S GREETINGS
AND HOW WE
HAVE ENJOYED THIS BRIEF MEETING
BUT NOW IT'S TIME
FOR THIS PANTOMIME
TO SAY "GOODBYE".

(*LXQ.77; FSQ.17C*)

(Final curtain.)

OPTIONAL "SLOSH" SCENE

The following is a section which can be added – if you want it. It's very messy and adds to the overall running time but the kids (of all ages) love it. It fits in at the end of Act Two, Scene One as:

THE JINI crawls off on all fours.

TWANKEE: Let's go and have a look inside. I can't wait to see my boudoir. (*Stopping them as they move directly towards it.*) I think we'd better go this way . . .

(T*hey all about-turn and face out front, producing torches as the lights fade to blackout. They creep down into the auditorium, shining torches around.*)

TWANKEE: Why is it so dark?

ALADDIN: You forgot to ask for windows, Mother . . .

TWANKEE: Oh well, Big Yin can always put them in later.

ALADDIN: Where are we now, d'you suppose?

TWANKEE: Looks like the ballroom . . . Don't reckon much to it. Needs a woman's touch . . . And some of these statues are no oil paintings . . .

ALADDIN: Look at that one . . .

TWANKEE: Whistler's father . . .

ALADDIN: Where's Wishee?

TWANKEE: Wishee?

(*Toilet flushes in the distance.*)

TWANKEE: Sorry I asked.

(*A banging up in the gallery.*)

TWANKEE: Hey! What's going on up there?

VOICE: 'S alright, mate. Just stripping some of this lead off the roof.

TWANKEE: D'you mind? We haven't even moved in yet . . .

ALADDIN: *(Leading back onto the stage)* I think there's something this way, Mother . . .

TWANKEE: I can't see a thing . . .

ALADDIN: Yes. There's a sign here. It says: WIDOW TWANKEE'S BOUDOIR. And there's a light switch.

TWANKEE: Well, switch it on, dear, let's have a shufti.

(Lights up to reveal:)

WIDOW TWANKEE'S BOUDOIR.

A bare box of a room with cracked plaster and lath showing through. This has been set up while they were in the auditorium and is a "three-fold" of hinged flats. There will need to be a tarpaulin on the floor for clearing with speed.

TWANKEE and WISHEE stand R. TWANKEE wears an overall wraparound and WISHEE a boiler suit. Both wear bowler hats. There is a small hole in the crown of WISHEE'S bowler. This last is a very quick change carried out during the torches section.

Props: Trestle table, step ladder, roll of wallpaper, folded wallpaper, paste brush, bowl of slosh and six plastic buckets. Blue bucket: has no bottom. Brown bucket: has small hole. The Yellow, Green and White buckets contain slosh. The Red bucket contains thin slosh.

TWANKEE: So this is Cell block H.

ALADDIN: Never mind, Mother. The Jini will soon make it nice for you.

TWANKEE: Jini nothing. We're going to decorate this ourselves. *(To the AUDIENCE.)* Oh yes we are.

ALADDIN: Well, I must go and find the Princess. *(Going.)* See you later.

TWANKEE: Typical. You mention shift work – he shifts.

(She crosses the room and slips C.)

TWANKEE: Watch out for that.

(*WISHEE crosses and slips in the same place.*)

TWANKEE: I told you to watch out for that. Well, Wishee. What do you think of my room as a whole?

WISHEE: As a hole, it's fine. As a room, it's rubbish.

TWANKEE: We'll soon sort that out. I see it as a lavish dose of Art Decorals with a touch of Texas Homecare . . .

WISHEE: (*Sucking his finger*) Ooo . . . I've got a splinter in me finger.

TWANKEE: I told you not to scratch your head. Now, we've got to put the paste on the paper and paste the paper on the walls so let's make a start. (*Picks up blue bucket.*) Fill me up, there's a dear.

WISHEE: Okey-cokey. Here we go.

Music: NARCISSUS.

(*WISHEE takes the yellow bucket and pours it into the blue bucket. It goes straight through and all down TWANKEE.*)

TWANKEE: You've gone and wet my knickers.

WISHEE: It's not my fault if you've got no bottom.

TWANKEE: Don't be personal. (*Taking brown bucket – with finger over hole.*) Here. We'll try this one.

(*WISHEE takes the red bucket and fills up the brown bucket.*)

TWANKEE: Here we go then. (*She crosses towards the ladder, slips.*) Watch out for that.

(*WISHEE crosses and slips.*)

TWANKEE: (*Climbing the ladder*) I told you to watch out for that.

WISHEE: Ooo look, your tights are all wrinkled.

TWANKEE: Are they?

WISHEE: Oh no they're not – it's your legs.

(TWANKEE *stands on top of the ladder and surveys the job. She takes her finger off the hole and the bucket "pees" slosh onto WISHEE. He gets the blue bucket to catch it but it goes straight through so he puts his bowler hat under and it fills up with slosh.*)

WISHEE: Finished?

TWANKEE: Nearly. (*Shakes out the last drop.*) What a relief. Now, let's get this paper hung . . .

WISHEE: Right. Just you be careful coming down that ladder. (*He absent-mindedly puts his hat on. Slosh runs down his face.*) Oh . . . I'm all pasty!

TWANKEE: (*Crosses, slips*) Watch out for that . . . (*Taking a roll of wallpaper.*) Now . . . got to put the paste on the paper. (*She unrolls the paper, takes the brush from the bowl and goes to paste but the paper rolls up again and she pastes the table. Repeat. Repeat. With great difficulty, she gets her heel onto table holding down one end of paper. She stretches it out and tries to surprise it with the brush but it rolls up again. She unrolls it.*) Would you please place your pinkie on my paper?

WISHEE: Where?

TWANKEE: Just there.

WISHEE: Right. (*He holds the wallpaper flat with one finger. She pastes the paper, at last pasting WISHEE'S hand. WISHEE glares. TWANKEE pastes up his wrist, then up his arm. She looks at the AUDIENCE.*) Shall I?

AUDIENCE: Yes.

(*TWANKEE tickles with the brush under WISHEE'S armpit.*)

WISHEE: Ah! Will you gerroff? You're doing that all wrong, you know.

TWANKEE: All wrong? I'll have you know I've got an ology in wallpapering.

WISHEE: The paste's on the wrong side, you silly sausage. It should go underneath.

TWANKEE: Underneath?

WISHEE: Underneath.

TWANKEE: Oh, underneath . . . (*She kneels down and pastes the underside of the table.*)

WISHEE: Honestly!

TWANKEE: Now then . . . Now to hang the paper.

(*TWANKEE takes the paper by the top corners and carries it in front of her towards the ladder, slips.*)

TWANKEE: Watch out for that.

(*She mounts the ladder, walking up the wallpaper and ripping it to pieces, ending up with a tiny fragment which she sticks carefully at the top of the wall.*)

TWANKEE: That's what they call piece work.

WISHEE: Look, come down.

TWANKEE: Come down?

WISHEE: Come down. You've got no idea. (*WISHEE picks up the green bucket, puts it on his shoulder, slips.*)

TWANKEE: I told you to watch out for that.

(*As WISHEE climbs the ladder, the bucket tips further and further back until, as he reaches the top, it drops and falls over TWANKEE'S head. Slosh runs down her face.*)

TWANKEE: Oh . . ! Now look what you've done . . . (*Takes the bucket off her head.*) I'm all sticky . . . (*She places the bucket at the foot of the ladder.*)

WISHEE: (*Coming down the ladder*) You always were stuck up . . . Whoooaaa . . . ! (*He puts his foot in the bucket and skates off on it, arms waving, out of control, sinks into splits, painfully heaves up again with drumroll.*)

TWANKEE: Honestly! Where's your get up and go?

WISHEE: (*Squeaky*) It's got up and gone.

TWANKEE: (*She takes the folded paper and hold it up against him*) Now just hold this.

WISHEE: Okey-cokey. (*He holds it up in front of him, hiding from head to shins.*)

(*TWANKEE pastes his shoes then on up the paper until she gets to the crotch. She pauses and looks at the AUDIENCE. She paints a ring road round. WISHEE looks over the top. TWANKEE points upward. WISHEE looks up, TWANKEE quickly paints his crotch – he wriggles and giggles. TWANKEE carries on up and gets to his face.*)

TWANKEE: (*To the AUDIENCE*) Shall I?

AUDIENCE: Yes.

(*SHE dabs bits onto WISHEE'S face and ends up covering him. WISHEE screws up the paper and throws it on the floor. He stands TWANKEE in front of the table and picks up the white bucket. Puzzled, she looks at the AUDIENCE. He adjusts the top of her overall to receive the slosh.*)

WISHEE: Shall I?

AUDIENCE: Yes.

(*He empties the bucket of slosh down inside her overall, she stands shivering with arms folded (keeping the slosh in position). He mimes hitting the bulging overall.*)

WISHEE: Shall I?

AUDIENCE: Yes.

(*He does and a jet of slosh spurts upwards all over TWANKEE. He falls about laughing. TWANKEE steadies him and places him in front of the table. She take off his bowler hat and puts it in his hands. She picks up the bucket and fills his hat with slosh, patting out the last drops. He looks at the AUDIENCE, puzzled. She takes the hat from him.*)

TWANKEE: Shall I?

AUDIENCE: Yes.

(She places the hat on WISHEE'S head. She suddenly rams it down so that the slosh is forced up through the hole in the crown, spurting ten feet into the air.)

(Blackout.)

There are various kinds of patent "Slosh" on the market these days but we've never found anything to beat the old fashioned mixture which can be made thicker or thinner according to the demands of the routine. This is made by grating shaving soap into a bucket of cold water and whisking it up with the biggest food whisk you can find until it's the right consistency for the effect. It can be coloured using food colouring.

Just as anything to do with sausages owes its origins to Joey Grimaldi, so our slosh routines are contrived in loving memory of Charlie Cairolli who turned "slosh" into an art form and who delighted so many countless millions at Blackpool Tower Circus and on television.

Props List

PROLOGUE.

    Wand for THYLVIA.
    Map of the Mountains of Doom for ABANAZAR.

Scene One – PEKIN MUNICIPAL PARK.

    Large foam or latex Notebook and Pencil for PONG.
    Large plastic or foam Truncheons for PING AND PONG.
    Set of Manacles for PING.
    Set of Manacles for PONG.
    Laundry Basket containing assorted colourful Washing for WISHEE.
    Large, colourful Watering Can set beside the FALIAH DR.

The FALIAH is in a plant pot against the proscenium DR. Ideally, it has one large attractive flower and, in this scene, is worked as a puppet so that it can turn to look at the audience, hang its head shyly, etc. Each time it is watered, it grows so the head of it needs to be attached to fishing line running over a pulley at the top of the proscenium or tormentor and running down to a cleat at the back for the operator. It should eventually grow very tall (ten – twelve – fourteen feet) so there is a lot of stem and leaves folded into the plant pot.

    Very colourful and "Orientalised" Supermarket Trolley for WIDOW TWANKEE set off L.
    Contains: Teabag, Oxo Cube, Crisps and any other give-aways for the Audience.

A very long Clothes Prop (set off) with stuffed-glove Hand at one end (carbon fibre is ideal for this, if it can be obtained, as it is very light and allows the pole to be *very* long while still manageable for the actor).

Scene Three – WIDOW TWANKEE'S LAUNDRY.

The main door is UC and, above it, is a sign proclaiming "Widow Twankee's Laundry" which can light up and flash.

A large, colourful Mangle set against a wall in which is a trap or flap for WISHEE to escape through (head first – so he might be glad of a mattress set behind). The rollers need to be thickly foamed to avoid actually flattening the actor and the top one runs in a vertical slot, allowing it to move up and down as WISHEE goes through. The bottom roller is directly turned by the handle and the top one turns because (apart from when WISHEE is going through) it rests on the bottom one.

A large and colourful Washing Machine. This is a front-loader with a door large enough for PONG to be apparently thrown in with the washing. There is a hatch on the top to take the powder, any number of knobs and settings and a huge Main Switch. The door has a perspex porthole so that we can see PONG. The "Water" is a sheet of polythene which the actor can raise and either set on hooks or lift up and down for tidal effects. If there is a rostrum or "bed" at the appropriate height set inside the machine, the actor can spin and contort as required.

> A large Packet of washing Powder labelled "BRAND X" is set on top of the machine.
> A Washing Line (with some washing already on it – set not to mask any action) is stretched across from on wing flat to the opposite wing.
> Clothes Pegs fixed to the Washing Line with one detatchable for TWANKEE.
> A long Bench is set below this.
> A "Dolly Tub" with an old-fashioned Posser is set C and can be moved out of the way by TWANKEE when finished with. This contains several pairs of knickers: a huge pair for "Pavarotti", a tiny pair for "Ronnie Corbett", etc.
> WISHEE's Laundry Basket set off UC containing a small pink sock, a Nightshirt and a Boilersuit.
> A set of six Traffic Cones set off UC for PONG.
> A Gong and Beater set off UC for PING.
> PING's helmet has a flashing blue "Police" light (which he can switch on for the entrance and off again) on it for this scene.
> They both have Truncheons as before.
> A really grotesque "identikit" Picture of WIDOW TWANKEE for PING.
> A large Snuff Box for ABANAZAR containing Fuller's earth or similar
> A wet Hanky in a polythene bag "pocket" in TWANKEE's apron.
> A flat, life-sized cut-out WISHEE WASHEE set off behind the Mangle.

Scene Four – ON THE ROAD TO THE MOUNTAINS.

> A length of String for PONG (mental floss).
> Collabsible Truncheon for PONG.

Scene Six – THE CAVERN OF THE WONDERFUL LAMP.

Jewels and more jewels – hanging from the walls, heaped up on the rocks and on the floor, spilling out of sacks, jars and boxes, glittering in the crevices, even growing on trees. You really can't go too far.

> A hand shovel for ALADDIN to use to fill:
> Two large shoulder bags or haversacks with loose jewels.

The wonderful lamp. There will need to be a couple of doubles of it but this is the original and, although it's dirty, it should be very ornate while maintaining the traditional shape.

> A Sign on a pole – to peep round the prosc. – saying: "WUB IT".
> A large Pocket Calculator for THYLVIA.

Scene Seven – A STREET IN PEKIN.

> Ukele for WISHEE. (He doesn't necessarily have to be able to play this and can mime to the orchestra pit but it's a nice chance to show off. If the actor plays something else, the line can be adjusted:

"When I'm sad and all alone,
I always play my saxophone/xylophone/Sousaphone"
Or:
"Often when I'm feeling blue,
I play this tune on my old Kazoo" (and so on and so on . . .)

Scene Eight – WIDOW TWANKEE'S KITCHEN.

> A large Table with a cloth reaching to the floor (to mask all the props stacked underneath).
> A huge Welsh Dresser. This is double-sided and revolves so that the JINI (and later JASMINE) can be transported round on it at speed.
> A large Cooker – large enough for ALADDIN to be inside it and able to get out gracefully.
> WIDOW TWANKEE'S Apron hanging on a peg on the Welsh Dresser. This has flaps which are velcroed and which TWANKEE can open.
> An Apron and a Chef's Hat for WISHEE hanging on another peg on the Welsh Dresser. The hat has a pig-tail attached.

A huge, thick Recipe Book set on the Table. This is covered with Fuller's earth for dust.
A large Bowl set under the Table.
A Tin containing very large metal Nuts (as in nuts and bolts) set under the Table.
A very large Oil Can set under the Table.
A Plastic Flower set under the Table.
A huge Flour Shaker containing Flour set under the Table.
A Water Pistol set under the Table.
A Box of Eggs set under the Table – containing three real eggs and one pot egg.
Two Plates (one gets broken) set on the Table.
A Tea Towel set under the table – this is to mop up mess as necessary.
A huge foam Hammer set under the Table.
A Tray of trick Sausages set under the Table. One sausage is "alive' and rears up – operated by WISHEE pulling a length of string or fishing line.
A Gun – preferably a Dirty Harry Magnum, firing one blank cartridge set under the Table. The bang could be done by the percussionist if the audience are nervous.
A huge and beautiful finished Birthday Cake with electric candles and a switch for TWANKEE.
A Cup and Saucer for TWANKEE – made of latex so that the actor can scrunch it up in his hand and it will spring into shape when released.
A Book for JASMINE set off behind the Welsh Dresser.

ACT TWO

Scene One – PEKIN MUNICIPAL PARK.

Chinese parasol for TWANKEE.
Very large and vulgar jewelry for TWANKEE.

The Growing Palace: This is a series of cut-outs – central building, two wings, two towers, two more towers, the peacocks, the fountain – and ending with some local landmark – to remind WIDOW TWANKEE of her real home. They slide up (and stay) individually from behind the ballustrade and foliage UC to collectively make the most opulent building.

Laundry Basket full of lamps – all similar to the magic one but new and shiny – plus a large rubber torch for ABANAZAR off L.
A collection of assorted old lamps for the PEKINESE to trade – table lamps, coach lamps, Kelly lamps, old torches, Wee Willy Winkie candlesticks, etc.
Police lamp for PONG to trade.
Standard lamp with fringed shade for TWANKEE.
Photograph for TWANKEE.

Scene Two – THE IMPERIAL PRISON

Manacles (as before) for PONG.
Sign on pole to appear round DR prosc. saying "WUB YOUR WING".
"Zoom" Ice-lolly for THYLVIA.

The Magic Carpet: This can be done in a variety of ways. At its most elaborate, it is suspended from a pair of clamped tab-tracks so that it can track and fly at the same time. In this event, it's good to rig the lamp which lights it to the mechanism so that it moves with the carpet and avoids lighting the wires. If this can't be done, a black-clad table can be trucked on with the carpet on top of it and trucked off with ALADDIN on it. If necessary, it can land off stage and not be seen at all.

Scene Three – THE DUNGEON OF ALADDIN'S PALACE (NOW IN THE SAHARA).

A Dungeon Wall flat which has three pairs of manacles apparently attached to it. In fact, the chains of these run separately through holes in the flat and have sandbags attached to the other end to take up the slack and each actor is in control of his or her own destiny though it should seem that they are joined so that, when WISHEE is being very dramatic and lunging forward, the other two are frequently wrenched back against the wall until they shout "Oh shut up!" and pull forward, hauling WISHEE back.

Ideally there is a trap centre stage with a hinged grating over it and steps leading down to substage but, if this can't be managed, there could be a barred cage on either R or L to contain "The Thing".

The "Thing" is simply the most horrible collection of long tentacles, claws, eyes on stalks, etc, which can be assembled so that the actual nature of the beast baffles description. A smoke gun is quite handy here – for it's breath.

A huge Spider which drops from the flies (as though on a bungee) and disappears upwards again. This needs to be foam as it hits ABANAZAR on the head.

The Lamp for this scene needs to be a soft (latex?) replica to play rugby with.

Scene Four – A STREET IN OLD PEKIN.

>A lightweight Easel for THYLVIA to drag on, with large cards on it bearing the messages on large cards.
>A large Broadsword for the EMPEROR.

Scene Five – PEKIN MUNICIPAL PARK.

>A large claw or tentacle from "The Thing Down There" which can velcro round ABANAZAR'S neck.
>A Broadsword for ABANAZAR.
>A long, green Tentacle (apparently) from the Failiah, which reaches out and (apparently) seizes ABANAZAR'S wrist.
>A second Tentacle could hook round his neck.

Suggested Lighting Cues

ACT ONE

Cue	Effect
1	Light area DL – sinister – for ABANAZAR.
2	Light area DR – pink and pretty – for THYVIA.
3	Lose area DL.
4	Light Pekin Tableau behind Gauze.
5	Full light for Opening Number as Gauze flies out.
6	Build for final Chorus of Opening Number.
7	Bright sunny day – for comedy.
8	Very romantic for ALADDIN/JASMINE duet and dance.
9	Return to state of LXQ.7.
10	Brighten for TWANKEE'S entrance.
11	Very colourful (pulsing?) for TWANKEE and PEKINESE song.
12	Snap B.O.
13	Evening, romantic (*Front Cloth*).
14	Snap B.O.
15	Interior, TWANKEE'S laundry – bright day.
16	Very colourful for "commercial" – with flashing lights (chasers?).
17	Return to state of LXQ.15.
18	Snap B.O.
19	Front Cloth – evening – dramatic.
20	Very colourful for "Wish Me Luck".
21	Very romantic sunset.
22	The sun actually does set – taking about 10 secs over it – to B.O.
23	Very sinister and dramatic – could be helped by dry ice. If there's a cyclorama or sky cloth, a couple of "Cloud" FX projectors could earn their keep during the next four cues (and, possibly during storm cues in Act Two).
24	The gloom darkens further suddenly – with lightning – and then restores to state of LXQ.23.
25	Both of these cues could be fairly wild flashes, lights up and down on.
26	Those parts of the set not moving – or moving majestically – flashes of lightning – general pandemonium – all trying to take the audiences' eyes away from those bits of the scene change we'd rather they didn't see.
27	Flashes of light on ALADDIN and ABANAZAR.
28	The Cavern of the Wonderful Lamp – very mysterious and glittery

29	Brighten the lower level as ALADDIN climbs down.
30	Dark and sinister as the entrance to the Cavern is sealed.
31	Reduce further – mysterious – for song.
32	JASMINE appears behind the gauze "rockface" and joins in.
33	THYLVIA appears behind another gauze part of the rock and also joins in.
34	Return to state of LXQ.30.
35	Lights down (with pyro-magic) and up again to somewhat brighter for THYLVIA's appearance.
36	Another "magic" down and up with pyro as ALADDIN vanishes.
37	Very colourful and glittery for THYLVIA'th THONG.
38	Snap B.O.
39	Street – Front Cloth – Evening.
40	A little brighter for start of song.
41	Very bright and jolly – rave – pulsing.
42	Fade to state of LXQ.40.
43	Cross-fade as Cloth flies out to light TWANKEE'S Kitchen – very bright for comedy routine – include Failiah.
44	Another magic down and up with pyro to magic the JINI on.
45	Yet another as above – this time JASMINE is magicked on.
46	Very colourful and dramatic for the start of Act One Finale.
47	Brighten the centre for the first chorus.
48	Even brighter for the second (and final) chorus.
49	Fade FOH lighting as Curtain falls – leaving tableau on stage.

ACT TWO

50	Behind the Gauze – very pretty Chinese scene – dancing, kites, perhaps a dragon?
51	Light for THYLVIA DR.
52	Light for ABANAZAR DL.
53	Lose ABANAZAR light DL.
54	Gauze flies out – bright sunny day.
55	Down and up with pyro to magic on the JINI.
56	Slow fade to evening – adding Chinese lanterns.
57	Cod romantic – for TWANKEE/ABANAZAR duet.
58	Return to state of LXQ56 – perhaps a little brighter.
59	This depends on where the JINI is coming from. If he's coming up on a lift trap then the cue is probably superfluous. However, if he's coming on from the wings, he will need a down and up with the pyro.
60	Very dramatic and threatening – lightning, etc.

61	The storm gets worse and more tumultuous.
62	Very gold, rich and dramatic for the EMPEROR.
63	Single Spot on the EMPEROR DR and Prison Bar Gobo spot on ALADDIN DC.
64	Lose the EMPEROR spot – widen the prison area for ALADDIN.
65	Light for Magic Carpet – avoiding wires if it actually flies.
66	Fade to B.O.
67	The Dungeon – very dramatic but bright enough for comedy.
68	Green sinister light up through the grill – shadows of waving claws.
69	Fade to B.O.
70	Street – front cloth – evening.
71	Cross fade as front cloth flies out – revealing the Park – evening.
72	Down and up – with pyro – for JINI entrance.
73	Bright for celebration – firework effects across the sky?
74	Snap B.O.
75	Street Front Cloth – bright day.
76	Cross fade as Front Cloth flies out to Emperor's Palace for Walkdown and Finale.
77	Lose FOH as Curtain falls – leaving onstage tableau.

Follow Spot Plot

ACT ONE

Cue	Effect – Stage L Follow	Effect – Stage R Follow
1		Pick up ABANAZAR DL and follow.
2	Pick up THYLVIA DR and follow.	
1A		Snap B.O.
2A	Fade B.O.	
3	Pick up ALADDIN UC and follow.	Pick up ALADDIN UC and follow.
3A	Cross to WISHEE UC and follow.	Cross to WISHEE UC and follow.
3B	Cross to JASMINE UC and follow.	Cross to JASMINE UC and follow.
3C	BOTH Open "Letterbox" to cover principals.	
3D	Snap B.O.	Snap B.O.
4	JASMINE and ALADDIN C.	JASMINE and ALADDIN C.
4A	Snap B.O.	Snap B.O.
5	BOTH pick up TWANKEE from entrance L and follow (inc. auditorium).	
5A	Snap B.O.	
6	JASMINE C and follow.	ALADDIN C and follow.
6A	Snap B.O.	Snap B.O.
7	TWANKEE and WISHEE C.	TWANKEE and WISHEE C.
7A	Snap B.O.	
8	BOTH pick up ALADDIN C (include WISHEE, ABANAZAR, PRINCESS, TWANKEE, PING and PONG as necessary and possible during the number) at ALADDIN'S exit, cross to JASMINE.	
8A	Fade B.O.	Fade B.O.
9	ALADDIN C.	ALADDIN C.
9A	Fade B.O.	
10	THYLVIA C.	THYLVIA C.
10A	Snap B.O.	Snap B.O.
11	WISHEE C.	WISHEE C.
11A	BOTH Open and "Letterbox" for Principals.	
11B	BOTH wild searchlight pinspots.	
11C	Fade B.O.	
12	ALADDIN C.	JASMINE C.
12A	BOTH Open and Letterbox for Principals	
12B	Fade B.O. with Curtain.	Fade B.O. with Curtain.

ACT TWO

13   THYLVIA D.R.
14   ABANAZAR D.L.
14A   Snap B.O.
13A Fade B.O.
15   ALADDIN C. (include JASMINE as possible).
15A FADE TO B.O.
16   TWANKEE and ABANAZAR C.
16A FADE B.O.
17   TWANKEE and follow through SONGSHEET.
17A Cross to pick up CAST UC for CALLS – Letterbox for FINALE.
17B FADE B.O. with TABS.

SOUND PLOT

Cue	Effect
1	Crack of Thunder.
2	Crack of Thunder.
3	FAILIAH: Squeaks – sounds a bit like "Hello".
4	FAILIAH: Squeaks – impressed by Audience.
5	FAILIAH: Squeaks – very coy and shy.
6	FAILIAH: Squeaks – terrified.
7	Washing Machine explodes into life and then gurgles and clanks through routine.
8	Washing Machine Belches (to mix with SQ.7).
9	Washing Machine clanks, bangs and dies (to mix with SQ.7).
10	Door creaks open (if there is a string bass in the pit, this is best done live by the musician).
11	Cold Wind, cawing Rooks, howling Wolves.
12	Crack of Thunder.
13	Huge Crack of Thunder into Hurricane and more Thunder (to cover Transformation into Cavern).
14	Rumble of Thunder.
15	Crack of Thunder.
16	Crack of Thunder.
17	Prolonged Hurricane with Thunder.
18	Interior of Dungeon – echoey dripping of water.
19	Savage Roaring, Grunting, Snorting and Snuffling – sounds of the unimaginable "Thing Down There".
20	Another burst of noise from the "Thing".
21	The "Thing" triumphant, seizing its prey (ABANAZAR) and fighting – goes on for about two minutes).
22	Diving Aircraft (Stuka?) ending in great crash and final tinkle.
23	Crack of Thunder.
24	FAILIAH: Squeaks, hurt – "Ouch".
25	FAILIAH: Squeaks – triumphant.

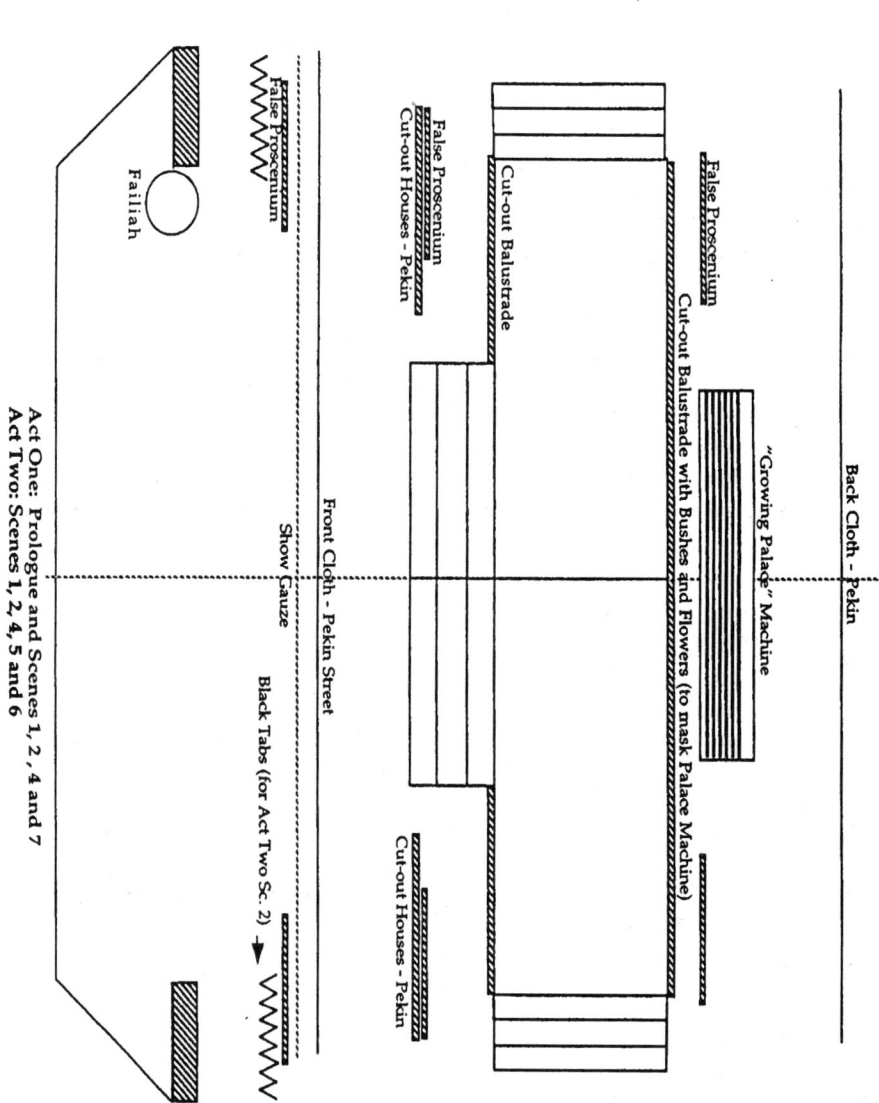

ALADDIN

Back Cloth - Pekin

"Growing Palace" Machine

Cut-out Balustrade with Bushes and Flowers (to mask Palace Machine)

Cut-out Balustrade

False Proscenium

Cut-out Houses - Pekin

False Proscenium

Front Cloth - Pekin Street

Show Gauze

Black Tabs (for Act Two Sc. 2)

Cut-out Houses - Pekin

False Proscenium

Failiah

Act One: Prologue and Scenes 1, 2, 4 and 7
Act Two: Scenes 1, 2, 4, 5 and 6

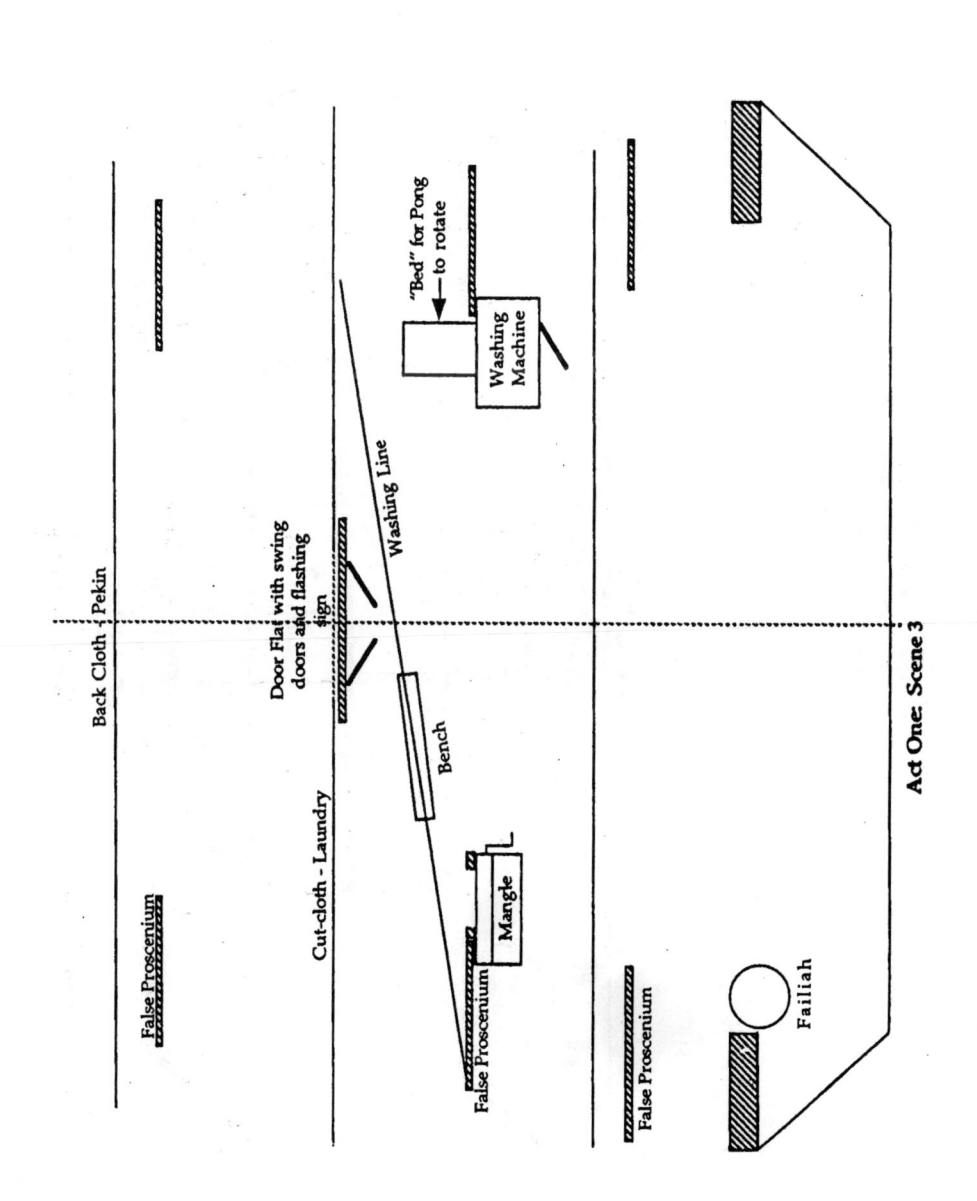

ALADDIN

Act One: Scene 3

- Back Cloth - Pekin
- False Proscenium
- Cut-cloth - Laundry
- Door Flat with swing doors and flashing sign
- Washing Line
- "Bed" for Pong to rotate
- Washing Machine
- Bench
- Mangle
- False Proscenium
- False Proscenium
- Failiah

98 ALADDIN

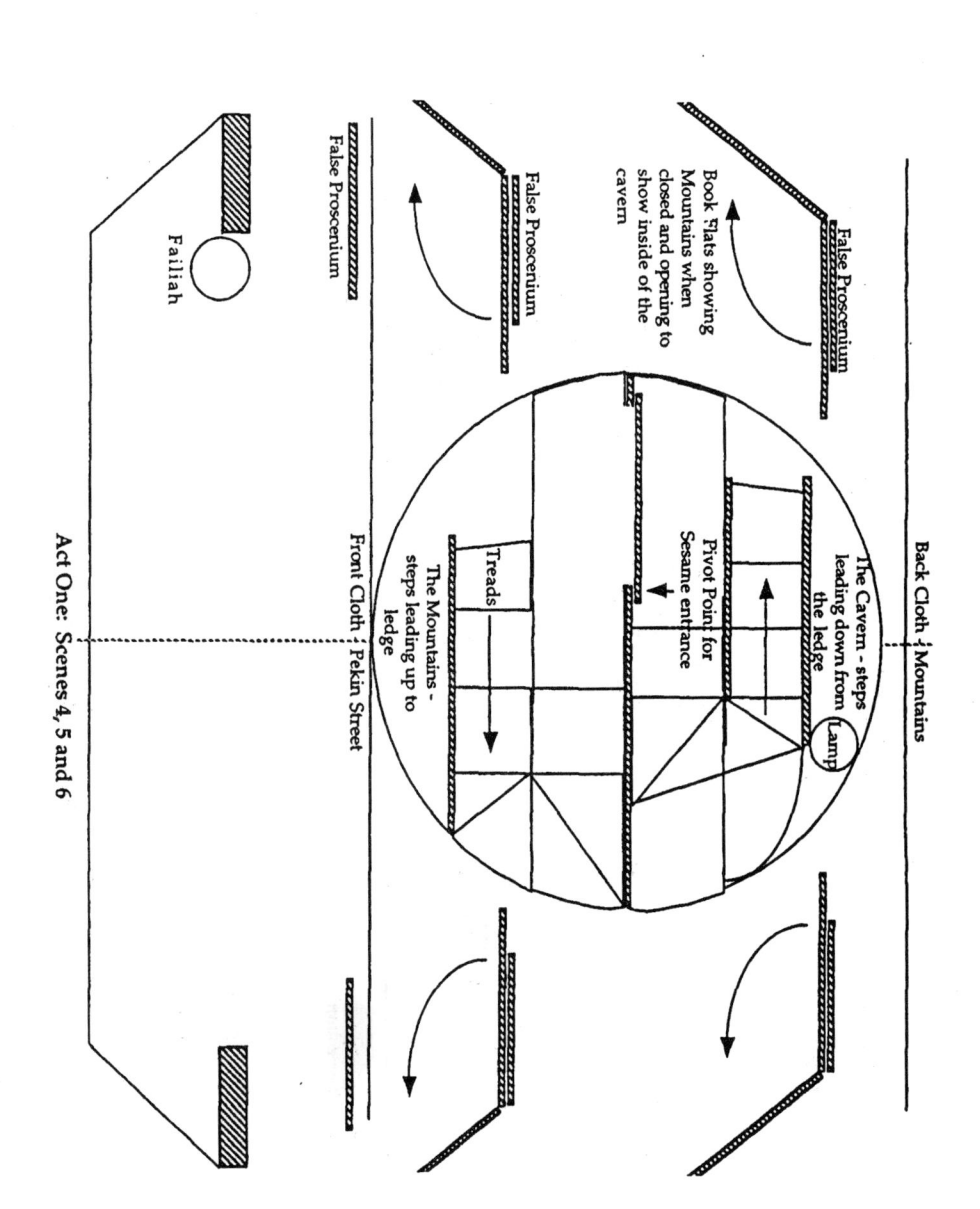

Act One: Scenes 4, 5 and 6

Diagram labels:
- Back Cloth / Mountains
- False Proscenium (multiple)
- Book flats showing Mountains when closed and opening to show inside of the cavern
- Failiah
- Front Cloth / Pekin Street
- The Cavern - steps leading down from the ledge
- Pivot Point for Sesame entrance
- Treads
- The Mountains - steps leading up to ledge
- Lamp

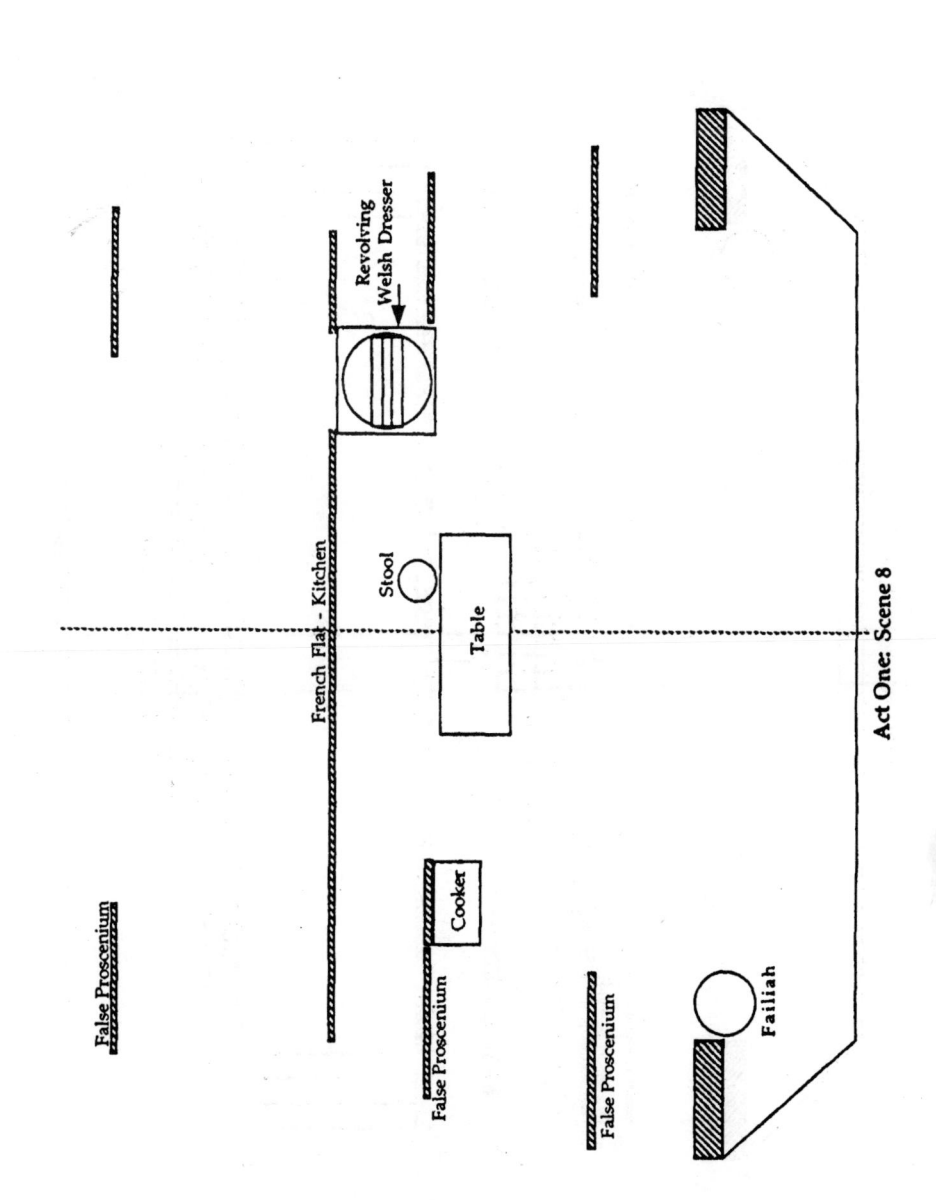

ALADDIN

99

Revolving Welsh Dresser

French Flat - Kitchen

Stool

Table

False Proscenium

False Proscenium

Cooker

False Proscenium

Failiah

Act One: Scene 8

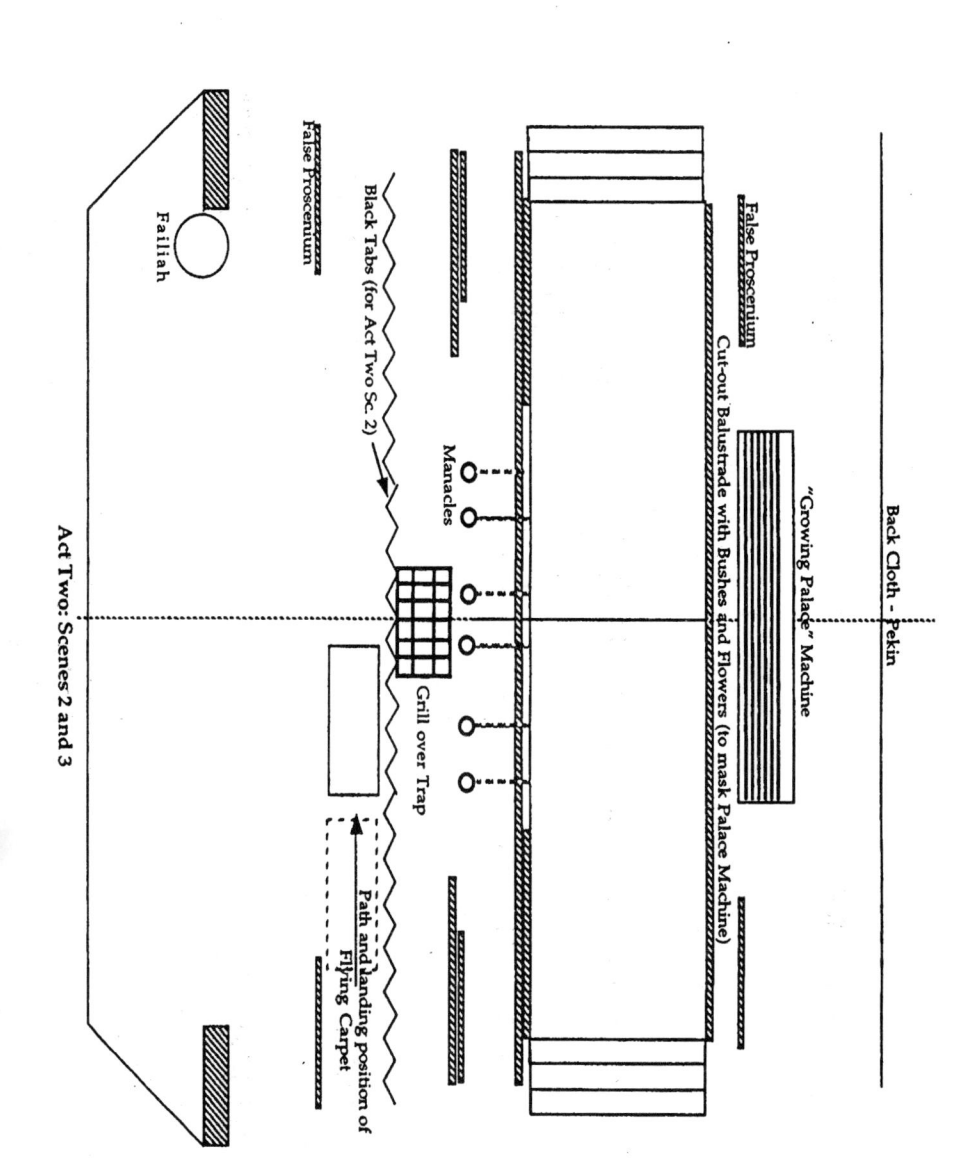

ALADDIN

Act Two: Scenes 2 and 3

- Back Cloth - Pekin
- False Proscenium
- "Growing Palace" Machine
- Cut-out Balustrade with Bushes and Flowers (to mask Palace Machine)
- False Proscenium
- Black Tabs (for Act Two Sc. 2)
- Manacles
- Grill over Trap
- Path and landing position of Flying Carpet
- False Proscenium
- Failiah